HOPIE

AND THE
LOS HOMES
GANG

Where are you, Fernando? Where are you, Hopie and Rosie?

Where are you, Efren, Alfredo, Filas, and a thousand others?

You are walking the streets of East Los Angeles tonight, living in the shadow of danger and of death. At any moment a bullet may cut off your young life, a knife may maim or deform you.

While I was with you, I did what I could. I am still following you with my deepest concern.

But, whom can I find to take my place?

Also by Hilary Paul McGuire

HOPIE

AND THE
LOS HOMES
GANG

A GANGLAND PRIMER

Second Edition
with 2011 Afterward

Hilary Paul McGuire

CONTENTS

LIST OF PHOTOGRAPHS

**Photo 1 - Brother Hilary with Some of His NJTL Students
(Hopie Is Second from the Right.)**

INTRODUCTION

The evening News informs us of the latest death in Northern Ireland, but what does it tell us about the number killed at the same time in East Los Angeles?

Very little has been written in book form about the unique street gangs in that great city. You have heard of the Puerto Rican gangs of New York and the black gangs of Chicago, but unless you're among the 10 to 12 million people of Southern California, you probably have never heard of the Mexican-American street gang.

Perhaps you think that you can read this book as just another interesting story, that you won't need to become really concerned until the gangland graffiti show up on your own back fence.

I wouldn't recommend that you wait that long. But, if you do insist on waiting, you might as well not wait in ignorance. Here is your gangland primer.

Since most Mexican people are very religious you may be tempted to consider these gangs as a Church problem. But, long before Los Angeles County became statistically the Gang

Capital of the world, the problem had graduated from a religious concern to a general sociological headache.

A sociological solution may, however, rise from religion at times. Certainly the gentle hand of Christian principles would be preferable for all involved to the iron fist of society.

The social strata recognized by Mexican-Americans and the terminology used to describe them in the United States locations where many people of Mexican ancestry live, would be a study in itself. This book will give the reader a non-academic introduction to these strata in Southern California, but especially will it introduce him to the group called *cholos*.

The term "Mexican-American" is the most sophisticated and is used especially by those American citizens who are descendants of Mexicans and who want to identify with the general American culture. One who calls himself a "Chicano" is usually politically active in an effort to bring about legal assimilation of the Mexican descendant by the United States government.

"Wetback," "TJ," and "*cholo*" are slang terms used to denote various segments of the Mexican-ancestry population. Wetback and TJ refer to Mexican nationals living in the United States, but TJ is most common in California because of the high incidence of illegal immigration through the border town of *Tijuana* or its environs.

The *cholos* are the segment of society most treated in this book so I leave it to the reader to learn the meaning from the story below. Simply speaking, the *cholo* is a gang member far removed from the laws and customs of American culture even though many *cholos* are native born Americans.

When the *cholo* is willing to enter general American society, he gets a job or makes money by some less legal means and advances toward respectability by joining a car club. This is not to say that all car club members are former *cholos*, just that the car club image seems to appeal to the *cholo* when he is ready for a somewhat less violent existence.

Group identification is such a primary part of Mexican-American culture that if a male teenager has never been in a gang or a car club, he has, what I'd estimate as a likelihood of about 60 percent of having been a member of a social club. Members of such clubs often have jackets printed with their club names and meet frequently for dances and beer parties.

Finally, there are a vast number of people of Mexican descent who do not fit into any of these categories, nor want to. They would probably choose the term "Mexican-American" to apply to themselves though they would prefer just plain "American." And why not? If they were born in the United States, they're just as American as any of us except the American Indians. Certainly they would balk at being wrongly called Spanish-Americans, i.e., descendants of Spaniards.

When people of Mexican ancestry refer to the white population of the world, there is less stratification, but the terminology is again quite varied. Everyone has heard of the white man being called *gringo*, but that term is most often used by Mexican nationals. A Mexican-American or American Chicano as described above would be more likely to call the white man an "Anglo" or, in less sophisticated moments, with a slip into or at least a nod to his Spanish-speaking past, he will call the white man a *gabacho* or *gringo*.

But by far the most common current reference to the white man, used by almost all strata of the Mexican descendants, is the term "paddy." That word is seldom used when a Mexican descendant faces a white man in conversation except in friendly joking or as an outright insult. Mostly it's used in conversation among themselves to refer to absent whites.

Everyone is afraid of the *cholos*. They are subject to neither the law of God nor the law of man. Most people just try to avoid them. But the gangs are permeating much of Southern California. Everyone is affected, at least by the graffiti. Such gang scrawlings always tell a tale, but only to those who can decipher the message.

A corner building with a multitude of names, many of which have been X-ed out, is probably on a thoroughfare which is traveled by many gangs. A garage door or masonry wall with only a few names on it is an initial indication that a territory has been claimed by a passing gang member.

And what do the gang writings say? They don't contain the ordinary crudities found in bathrooms, the only place where most Americans have encountered graffiti. No, the *cholos* write at a minimum (more will be explained in the story below), their gang nicknames and the initials of their gang. So they are vandalizing property and boldly signing their names to it.

This is a personal account of my involvement with the gangs. I am a member of the Benedictines, (a Religious Order). My normal occupation is teaching and my favorite sport is tennis. A few years ago I was given an assignment in Los Angeles which led eventually to contact with the gangland youth of the area. At first I was tempted to shy away from them, but my understanding of Christianity stopped me.

Much of my story relates the reactions of people around me to my deepening involvement with gang members. My readers will, no doubt, also have a great variety of reactions. *The reaction I most want to elicit is one of involvement.* Too many of us are arm-chair experts.

Mentioned in the story is Brother Modesto, also a Religious Order member, who does work somewhat similar to my own. As of this writing, he is at Our Lady of Soledad Church, East Los Angeles.

Brother Modesto's thesis, as well as my own, is that ordinary religious instruction will never reach the thousands of gang kids who, far from practicing religion, aren't even practicing good citizenship. If one is not even a law-abiding citizen, in a country where the laws are basically designed to help people respect other people, he certainly isn't going to be a religious person. It's necessary to help the kids fit into society before one can expect even rudimentary Christianity.

Photo 2 - Brother Modesto with Some of His Boys

All good citizens should be able to identify with such goals.

Working with unruly kids is, as Brother Modesto points out, a risk to any individual or institution, even to the Church, but he says (and I concur wholeheartedly), "We're nothing if we're not available."

He figures the drop-out rate of gang members from high school is about 50 percent and tries to counter the resultant problems by setting up tutoring programs in the various neighborhoods. Often a gang member drops out because he doesn't dare appear at a school where a rival gang holds dominance.

Without an education the kids can't even read and spell well enough to fill out job applications. What future is there for a person who, in his late teens, is already scrounging for the same jobs which old, degenerate bums are seeking? Is it any wonder they turn to theft (either breaking and entering or robbing people on the street) to achieve some sort of subsistence?

Other ways of helping gangs he has devised include: making visits to parole officers to act as liaison between the police and juvenile offenders; giving lectures in Chicano studies to college classes to promote understanding of the gang situation and to recruit tutors; having Masses and other religious activities right in the homes of the *cholos* (especially at the time of a funeral or on the anniversary of the death of a gang member); making friends with all factions in a school during lunch hours, and starting a community thrift show where clothing and furniture unwanted by one family can be passed on to a family which can use it.

He now wants to start a halfway house where kids in trouble with their parents can stay a few days while Brother or one of his helpers arbitrates. There has even arisen the idea of starting a new Order in the Church specifically dedicated to work with gang youth.

In short, the approach might be called "catechesis by availability."

The story of Hopie and the Los Homes Gang is my own application of that concept. May it help you to see how serious the problem is and move you to help with it.

1 THE CLASSES THAT WEREN'T

"Hey, Brother-man, give us a ride to the school."

Four Mexican-American teenagers wearing tank tops and sleek black, shoulder-length hair were hailing me.

"Oh Lord," I thought, "It's some of those rowdy gang kids." They were already opening the car doors so I tried hastily to gather my tennis equipment into heaps.

"Just up to the school, Brother," one of them said as they jostled their way into the car. "It's only a coupla blocks."

I didn't know what to say but the boys constantly shoved and poked each other and muttered in a combination of Spanish and English.

I glanced over my shoulder a couple of times to see that my equipment was safe. The boys were tossing my tennis balls about.

I pulled into the combination schoolyard and churchyard and raised the doors by remote control.

"Gee, how'd ja do that, Brother?"

I poked the button twice more for their benefit.

"Catch ya later, Brother-Man!" was their shrill thanks as they flopped out of the car.

"Whew," I sighed as the garage door slammed safely behind me.

Moments later I was unloading in my room when the phone rang.

"Brother," the rectory secretary said, "you'd better come and see these papers; some boys shoved them through the mail-drop."

"I can't imagine what they'd be," I said.

"They have your name on them and I don't like the looks of those boys."

I trudged out to the front desk.

Mrs. Sanchez, the secretary thrust a packet of wallet-sized papers and cards into my hand. I shuffled through them, puzzled as to where I had seen them last. Then I remembered.

"Good Lord, these came out of my billfold! Oh my gosh, I must have left my wallet on the seat of the car and those kids stole it!"

"Those boys are real trouble," Mrs. Sanchez moaned.

"After I was nice enough to give them a ride, they do this to me!" I glared fiercely. "I'm going after them."

"You'd better be careful, Brother," Mrs. Sanchez called after me. "One of them looked like the boy they call "Opie" or something like that. He's probably a member of the Li'l Valley gang.

I drove the streets, watching for a group of four boys. Gang graffiti marred every street-side wall. "Yes, this is certainly Li'l Valley territory," I thought, as I noticed the – LV- written under most nicknames.

In some places a nickname had been crossed out with a big X and a fresh new name added beside it. The name was "Hopie."

Could this be the boy I was chasing? I had become familiar with graffiti in my year of teaching mathematics at our East Los Angeles parish school, but today was my first real contact with the scribblers.

At a corner grocery store some 20-ish Mexican youths were busily painting a colorful mural over graffiti. I dashed into the store to look for my thieves. On the way out, I spoke to one of the painters. "Did you see four boys together, all about 14 years old?"

"Naw, man, we dint see nothin'."

Frustrated, I returned home.

The rectory bell rang for dinner. Four priests and I gathered around the table. Food made the rounds while Father Nolan, the Pastor, spoke to the youngest priest, a bespectacled 30-year-old. "Father Emrick," he said.

"Yes?"

"How about you and Brother Hilary organizing a junior high CCD class?"

Father Emrick looked over at me to see if I showed any serious objections. All I knew about teaching a religion class was that CCD meant Confraternity of Christian Doctrine. He shrugged his shoulders and said, "OK."

The Pastor continued. "You should be able to roust out at least 25 students from our list of about a thousand public school children."

"I'll start phoning right after s upper," I said.

Father Emrick looked puzzled. "Are we both going to teach at the same time?" he asked.

"Yes, you and Hilary can team-teach," said Father Nolan.

It was three days later. Father Emrick unlocked the door to the classroom building. Suddenly, two girls sauntered into the schoolyard in our direction. Then a shirtless boy whizzed through on his "banana"-seated bicycle. Another cyclist chased him. I shouted at them, "Are you guys coming to religion class?"

They jammed on the brakes just enough to peel a long strip of rubber off the tires and one screamed, "You gotta be kidding, Brother-man; we stood in school all day already. We barely got out just now."

Father Emrick wanted to start class promptly. "Let's go on in," he said to the girls.

"Can't we wait for a few others?" they pleaded.

Eventually a few others arrived, jousting boys and delightedly-watching girls. But the religion class was a flop! In the weeks following we tried different text-books, discussion groups, even films, but the attendance seldom exceeded ten. One large addition to our ranks, we felt we could do without.

"They're *cholos*, probably gang members too," warned a young boy as he stood beside me one day before class. We were watching a group of shirtless or tank-topped boys entering the yard.

"See how they walk with their arms going back. They cause all the trouble around here. Maybe they're the ones who stole your wallet, Brother."

In their "uniforms" they all looked the same to me. I ignored the reference to my lost wallet since I could never hope to find the exact thief. But, now that Felipe mentioned it, they did seem to walk strangely.

Their bent shoulders were slung back and their elbows were bent to the rear. A slight upward cupping of their palms and raising of their chins made their gait the epitome of defiance. It was more of a strut than a walk.

"What's a *cholo*?" I asked.

"Them's *cholos*, wearin' them beanies."

"Those beanies," I said in an effort to correct his English. "You mean those dark blue stocking caps?"

"Yeah, them's beanies."

"Don't you guys ever speak proper English?"

"Everyone talks this way, Brother."

"Not everyone, just here in East LA," I said pleadingly.

"That's all that matters to me, Brother."

Photo 3 - Some of Brother Modesto's Boys

I gave up and returned my gaze to the *cholos*. They had moved into a corner of the yard and were sitting on one of the schoolyard benches.

"What are they doing over there?" I asked. By this time other members of our class were arriving. One girl had heard my question and broke in with, "They're probably writing on the walls or sniffing."

"Let's get class started," said Father Emrick as he bustled onto the scene.

Felipe and I, and the girl who had just spoken followed Fr. Emrick. But, when we settled around the table most of the class was missing!

"Step out and see where the others are," I told Felipe.

He was back in a moment. "They've gone over to the corner."

Father Emrick scooted his chair back angrily. He stepped brusquely to the doorway and called the names of two of the more attractive girls. Nothing happened. "We'll just start without them," he said, returning to the table.

I went to the door. Sure enough, the wall-hugging boys had captivated the larger part of our class. Walking over to the huddle, I spoke quietly to a couple of our more faithful class members. Then I moved back toward the classroom. At the door I stopped to see if I had a following. None!

That's the way our class went for the next two weekly meetings. Finally we had a brain-storming session. Father Emrick asked our three or four pupils, "What can be done either to get rid of those guys or to bring them into the class?"

"Why don't you take us to the snow, Father?" it was Felipe speaking.

I didn't see the connection.

"What's that got to do with CCD class?" Father Emrick asked curtly.

"Well, you know that would bring more people to class and, besides, most classes have a trip once in a while. It never snows in LA."

We decided to try it.

2 COLD WATER—AND HOT!

It was an afternoon in December. A morning rain had wiped away the smog and dumped snow in the mountains. The clean air allowed long-distance communication. The mountains were speaking and youth could hear best. "Come to the snow," they begged.

The word had leaked out that our junior high CCD class was taking a trip. Our class-room was packed. Fifty "pupils" had shown up! Even the wall-huggers and suspected wallet-snatchers careened into the meeting room.

About fifteen of the total group appeared to be of the rowdy type which I had learned to associate with the neighborhood or barrio street gangs. This was more gang-like youth in one place than I had ever seen. The chill of the late afternoon had forced many of them to cover their sleeveless "muscle shirts" with a dark blue or brown plaid shirt.

Felipe sidled up to me. He tugged at my robe to win my attention in what was fast becoming a madhouse. "I don't know if this was such a good idea," he said.

"What do they call those shirts?" I asked, giving a chin-nod toward a bandana-crowned boy whose back was to me.

"Them's Pendletons."

"Don't they ever tuck in their shirt tails?"

"Oh, no, Brother; it's the style, man."

Father Emrick approached us. "Let's try to get something organized," he said rather hopelessly.

I nodded, reached for a notebook and tried to shout above the roar; "OK, OK, let's settle down!" A slight quieting ensued.

"Now, anyone who wants to go on this trip with us must sign his name. Give your address and phone number so we can know how to contact you." I asked for addresses because I had come to realize that many families did not have telephones. East Los Angeles, an unincorporated area sandwiched in by Los Angeles and her 75 or more suburbs, has the lowest per capita income in the United States.

"How're we gonna get there, Brother?" a voice asked.

"We'll rent a bus," I said, "but that'll take money."

"Let's have a carwash," someone suggested.

"Good idea. When do we start?"

"This Saturday," Felipe piped up. "I know a gas station where we can hold it."

"OK," I said, "Let's all meet here at 10 that morning."

As I finished speaking, I put the notebook and a pen on the table. Feeding starved chickens would not have caused more of a frenzy. As the teens scrambled to use the pen, Father Emrick tightened his lips and scowled at me. He picked up his catechism and Bible and started for the door. "I'm not having anything further to do with this," he growled.

I took one giant step backward and found myself against a wall and alone. What could I do? "I can't back out on these kids now," I told myself. Shrugging off the loss of support, I plunged into meeting my fate. Three *cholos* were waiting for a couple of others to finish signing the notebook. "You guys don't happen to have been among those hitch-hikers I picked up down on 6th Street a few weeks back do you?"

"Naw," came from several mouths. Then one guy added, "We heard you lost your wallet that day, Brother."

By this time others had joined us. One of the original group said to the new members, "Hey, guys, Brother thinks we might've been part of that bunch of mean old boys who heisted his wallet a coupla months back."

It was perfectly indicative of the brashness of the group that one little fellow, no more than about 12 years old, lowered his usual high voice and snorted, "We scored heavy, man." He knew the anonymity that their uniforms and nicknames give them. He was daring me to accuse them further.

I sought refuge in my friend Felipe. But he offered little encouragement. "Don't bother to look for their names on that sheet, Brother. Even if those guys signed the right names, you still wouldn't know what face to put with the names."

Nevertheless I studied the list and there, to my surprise, was not just the name, but the address and phone number of someone called "Hopie Lopez." Had he been in that group I spoke to? There was no way of telling.

Inside the rectory I showed the list to Mrs. Sanchez. "That might be his correct name," she said, "but the address and phone probably aren't right. Those boys are the devil to pin down."

She rolled her eyes and said, "You know, I've lived here all my life. There's been gang activity as long as I can remember, but it's constantly spreading and getting worse. In the '40s the *pachucos* just had knives and slicked-back hair, but now they call themselves *cholos* and they've all got guns and dope. And there are so many gangs. Why, I heard on the news the other night that Los Angeles County has about 300 major gangs, more gangs than any similar-sized area in the whole world!

"Hmmm," I said.

"And that's just the big ones, ones the police know about and which have more than about 50 members," she concluded.

I went slowly to my room and stretched out on the bed. What could I do? Teach religion to a bunch of thugs I could not even meet? And if I met them, then what?

"It seems to me," I thought, "that the main problem is that these kids are antisocial. Society and her laws are basically Christian so you can't expect to teach religion to anyone until you've helped him fit into ordinary society." I took that as my working hypothesis.

How distant my *cholos* were from ordinary society was to become more evident.

By Saturday Felipe, by no means a *cholo*, had convinced the owner of a service station that we should use his water and parking area. With about 15 prospective snow-trippers I was walking the several blocks to the station when it occurred to me that, though we had plenty of rags and buckets, we needed a sign.

"Don't we need a sign to announce our carwash?" I asked the group.

At once I was flanked by two of the shirtless *cholos*. "Don't worry about that, Brother; we've got our markers." They whipped out their marking sticks as though they were switchblades.

I nearly doubled over with laughter to think of these implements of vandalism being used in my service. "But we don't have anything to mark on," I said.

"Yes we do, Brother." We were passing a telephone pole and before I knew what they had in mind, they had ripped from the pole a fine cardboard poster announcing a Sunday afternoon dance called a *tardeada*.

"You can't take down someone else's sign," I objected.

"Too late now," one of them grinned.

Photo 4 - Car Wash

They pounced atop the poster like two cats, holding it to the ground. After a few deft strokes, they presented it to me proudly. In the finest gangland script, a bold, angular style, it read, "Carwash $1."

That tickled me. I wanted to get better acquainted but these boys weren't ready to tell me their names lest I turn them in for vandalism. So I listened to conversations all day until I finally attached the name "Hopie" to a small, extremely vibrant 14-year-old. His sign-making partner was his somewhat larger best friend, Fernando.

As the hours dragged on at our carwash, our hopes for a snow trip dimmed. Only about six people trusted their paint jobs to my crew. The lot was alive with kids crawling atop a retaining wall, sitting on curbs, and chasing around in circles. Many of them were more trouble than they were worth. They even rolled old tires into the street.

Trouble really started with a girl called Chica. She was one of the more attractive girls, so I asked her, "Please stand out on the curb and hold the car wash sign." I thought customers might be more likely to come in for her than for one of the boys.

"No," she snapped, "I want to be with the others." She pulled out a water gun and started to chase another girl. I caught her and jerked it away.

"You glass-eyed freak," screamed Chica's friend Rosie. Rosie deliberately produced another gun and squirted me. I grabbed the gun away and smashed it to bits on the pavement. As Chica sassed me mercilessly, I tried to stick a dripping rag into her mouth. She ran away crying.

"Why'd ja make her cry?" screamed Rosie.

"I just threw a wet rag at her like so many others today," I said.

I turned away and she spit at me. I whirled and slapped her on both cheeks. That was it! Everyone was against me! Rosie headed for home shouting, "I'm gonna bring my big brother back to beat the shit out of you!"

Stories I had heard of gang violence flashed into my mind. A man had once shouted at some boys for pulling at one of his trees as they walked across his lawn. They had shot him dead, right on his own front porch.

I was plenty scared, but I couldn't leave until I had cleaned up the mess. A full box of detergent lay scattered on the pavement. I begged Felipe to help me hose it away and a river of soap bubbles headed for the street while the *cholos* sat on a wall, dangling their bare feet over the side, and whispering jokes to each other. A couple of them flipped 5-inch switchblades into the air.

"Here comes Rosie's brother," someone shouted while Felipe and I feverishly gathered buckets and far-flung rags. Luckily for me, no one showed up! When Felipe and I started around the corner of the gas station out of sight of the mocking boys, Felipe said, "I'd better split home, Brother."

I could see his point and I too walked as fast as I could without seeming to run. The rectory was a long block away, but the kids had not decided what to do yet so it was a while before they came after me. When they did so, they came in a group.

They hailed me in a friendly fashion. Filas, an older fellow whom I had known for several months, called for a parley, "*Chale*, Brother, wait for us."

I returned a few steps to meet them and apologized for getting mad. Typical of the Li'l Valley gang of which I knew him to be a full-fledged member, Filas said; "You don't gotta apologize, Brother-man." Then he had the younger *cholos* help me carry the equipment to the rectory. They stayed in the yard to play while I went in for a shower.

Not convinced that they had all forgiven me so readily, I went out later to check the condition of the schoolyard. Not only were no light bulbs broken or doors bashed in, there were not even any new gang name scrawlings.

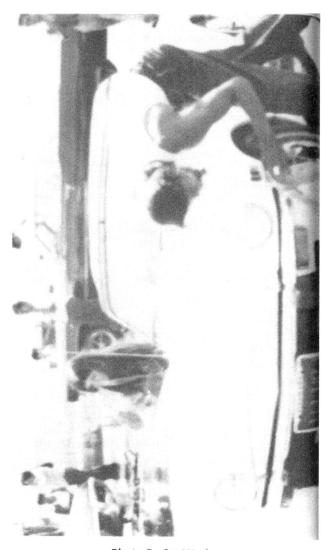

Photo 5 - Car Wash

3 "YOU'LL WISH YOU HADN'T"

"How'd the carwash go?" Father Nolan asked when we sat down for supper.

"Wild."

"That's all you can expect from these hoodlums," Father Emrick volunteered. Then he turned to Father Nolan. "Did you hear about the latest gang death?"

"Nope."

"Right over here at our friendly neighborhood junior high."

"What happened?" I said.

"Well, I don't know the particulars, but rumor has it that one of the 8th grade rowdies had an altercation with someone in another gang."

"Oh brother!" I thought.

"Well," Father Emrick continued, "it seems this youth sallied forth after school yesterday, a car roared past, and he fell dead—two bullets in his chest."

Not to be outdone in storytelling, Father Nolan began, "Did you hear the one about the Vietnam veteran who came home on leave?"

"He was walking down the Boulevard with a friend and someone drove past, shooting. The friend hit the deck, but the soldier, who had survived so much shooting in Vietnam, died on the streets of his own barrio."

We ate silently for a while

"So, Brother Hilary, you know what you're getting into when you deal with these gang brats."

"Yes, but somebody's got to help them. And besides, I've already promised them I'll take them to the snow so I can't back out now."

"Just don't say we didn't warn you," Father Nolan scowled.

After the meal I stepped out to stroll in the yard. I met a Mr. Romero who had seen part of our carwash show that day. "Have you met Brother Modesto?" he asked. "He works with the gang kids at the parish in the territory of the Maravilla gang—you know, the ones who come over here and cross out all the LV's and put HMV. That means *Hoyo* Maravilla."

"Yeah," I said, "but what's *hoyo* mean?"

"Oh *senor*," Romero replied in his best Mexican sing-song and I could feel he was about to make friendly fun out of my gringo status, "you don't know what is *El Hoyo*?"

"No."

"*El Hoyo* is The Hole," he said. "They call it that because the gang originated over here in a neighborhood where there's a little draw or valley."

"I see."

"You don't know much Spanish do you, Brother?" Mr. Romero seemed concerned.

"No."

"Maybe that's alright, though." His face lightened a bit. "If you knew any real Spanish, you still wouldn't understand this street language. Some people call it Spanglish or *pachucho*, but it's technically named *kalo*."

I looked interested.

"Some of it is due to the creativity of the people and, believe me, there's plenty of that, but much of it is from ignorance of spelling rules. For example, you've heard of the VNE gang?"

"Yes."

"You've heard that VNE stands for *Varrio Nuevo Estrada*, right?"

"Right."

"But the word is not spelled *varrio*; it's spelled *barrio*, the Spanish word for 'neighborhood.' But in Spanish the 'b' sounds like 'v' so these American born and educated kids spell it with a 'v'."

"I see; very interesting."

"Well, I gotta run, Brother, but you hang in there. Just don't get yourself killed."

"I will try not to."

"Oh, and Brother," he turned back as if he had thought of something important. "You gotta know what *puto* means; it's probably not in anyone's dictionary, but it's gotta be the most common word among these dudes. I know cuz I grew up right over here on Downey Road."

I nodded my head in expectation.

"You've seen it on all the walls haven't you, where one gang member has crossed out another?"

"Yes. Yes, what does it mean?"

"You've been around here how long now?"

"About a year, but I hadn't met a single *cholo* face to face until I began to plan a trip to the snow."

"Okay, okay. It means male whore….and *puta* is the female variety."

"Okay," I said, "I'll keep that in mind. Thanks for the lesson and I'll try to get together with Brother Modesto right away."

I phoned Br. Modesto. He said he had a short trip planned for his youth group in the coming week-end. Maybe I would like to take some of my kids along with him to the beach and to visit some peaceful gardens. I readily agreed, but when I mentioned peaceful gardens the next day to Hopie and some of his friends, they scornfully said, "That's duddy, Brother-man; we wanna go to the snow."

So only Felipe and two of the gentler girls made Br. Modesto's trip. About half an hour after our return home from the outing, Father Nolan came to my room.

"Your thugs haven't gone home yet; they're sitting on the back steps of the church sniffing paint."

When I went out to see, I was relieved to find that they were not part of the group I had taken with Br. Modesto. Those had apparently gone home to bed, tired after a full day of innocent activity. What I found was a group of four or five girls spraying paint into a paper bag, putting their noses in to inhale the fumes, and giggling all the while. They looked familiar to me. Perhaps they were part of my 50-member snow group?

They were obviously either gang members or gang sympathizers because they were wearing heavy black eye-makeup even though they were a mere thirteen or fourteen years of age. Of course the biggest clue to their gang sympathies was the fact that they were sniffing paint. Also, characteristic of the *chola*, was the fact that they were wearing jeans fitted like a pair of tights. Levis are what *cholas* wear about 99 percent of the time in public.

I could still recall Mrs. Sanchez telling me that paint fumes cause brain damage. So after a bit of chat, when one of the girls whipped out the can for another whiff, I grabbed it away.

"You chicken shit!" one of them shouted at me.

Another gasped, "Don't say that!"

The reply was, "I don't care; he's got our paint."

"Come on, man, we need it!"

"Why? It causes brain damage."

"I don't care; it's my brain."

Another girl added, "It makes you see pretty stars in your head—feels real good."

I stayed with them just long enough to catch some names. When I thought I had as many as I was going to get, I went to my room to see if these girls were on my list of prospective snow-trippers. Sure enough, there they were, all listed with the same phone. When I dialed, a man answered. He readily confided to me, as an interested church official, that the girls' mother had left him and that he could not control them.

4 DEATH—AND "LIFE"

Filas had the secretary call me from supper to give him a ride home. Filas was about eighteen, a high school dropout, didn't have a job, didn't want one, and was constantly high on either paint fumes or cheap wine.

His nickname, Filas, is just as physically appropriate as most Mexican-American nicknames. It means "rows of soldiers." The size of his frame and the intensity of his gang dedication must have made him very helpful in battle.

He was a full-fledged member of the long-established Li'l Valley Gang, belonging to the division called The Jokers. Yet he was enough of a loner to hang around with my younger *vatos*, as he called them, (meaning "dudes" in the sense of "fine fellows").

He had accepted my friendship more easily than any of the younger boys and had been so helpful in the carwash crisis that I gladly agreed to take him home. I asked Filas as we walked toward the car, "Do you wear that rosary around your neck for protection or something?"

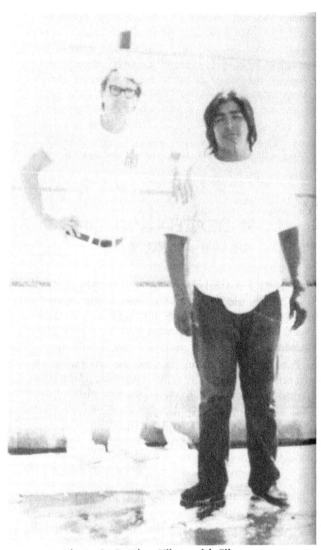

Photo 6 - Brother Hilary with Filas

"Nah," he said, "I like to put the plastic cross between my teeth and bite on it when I'm high on paint fumes. It makes me see stars and feel real good."

As I drove according to his directions, I said, "This isn't Li'l Valley territory is it? I thought you lived in the Valley."

"My family moved out, Brother."

"That's good. Now maybe you can quit the gang."

"Oh no, that's why I had to ask you for a ride home. These other dudes know me and I'd get killed walking home through foreign turf."

"And I suppose you must stay with the Valley guys for protection?"

"That's right. They'll back me up."

I groaned. "What a vicious circle," I said. "There's no way out unless you move far, and that sort of move would be too expensive."

"Yep," said Filas without a trace of regret.

When I had dropped him at his home I went off to a park to my favorite "class"; teaching tennis. Later I returned to the rectory and Mrs. Sanchez called me out to the front desk. It was Filas again. This time he was with handsome Big James who had the habit of signing his name on walls as *El James*, as though he were the one and only. Jesse was there too and I thought how fittingly reminiscent of Jesse James these boys were when they were together. They were older members of my snow trip crew, both about 15.

There seemed to be an air of dread suspense about Filas as he motioned me into one of the little offices where he knew we consult with people. It was more: a sense of urgency, desperation, and a call for moral support.

Suddenly he was trembling as he tried to speak: "Blackie, my brother—in my arms. Dead."

By now he was shuddering violently. I turned to Big James who said, "You probably didn't know his brother Blackie, but he just died tonight, not an hour ago—in Filas' arms."

23

Jesse took over. "They were driving down the Boulevard and Blackie wanted to buy some sniffing paint. His mother didn't want him to, but Blackie was driving so he pulled over."

The pulsation of Filas' sobbing body made me glance his way. I could do nothing so I looked back to Jesse.

Big James broke in. "That store is the best one for buying paint, you know, but it's in VNE territory. Filas spotted these VNE dudes when Blackie went in. When he was almost ready to come out, Filas saw a gun. He shouted at Blackie. Blackie jumped behind a Volkswagen, but the dudes ran around shooting about eight shots. They got Blackie in the head."

A stark silence set in, punctuated by Filas' gasps through quivering lips.

"Let's walk outside," I said, "we can sit on the church steps."

"We've already been there," said Jesse. "We came in just to let you know, Brother."

I put my arm gently around Filas' huge shoulders as he stumbled for the door. We took the few paces to the church steps in the moist night air.

"We want to be alone now, Brother," said Big James.

The next night Filas came to me, about ten in the evening, and very imbued with paint fumes. I had only recently learned that the most popular current method of getting high on paint is not so much spraying it into a paper bag and inhaling the bag's air, but spraying it onto a thickly-folded handkerchief and sucking air through the handkerchief into the mouth.

Filas' every breath smelled thickly of paint fumes as he sobbed copiously for about twenty minutes beside me on a sofa. Perhaps it would have helped if I had hugged him and let him blubber into my shoulder, but this boy was nearly 200 pounds and bigger than I am in every dimension. I took it as my function simply to listen to his recital of grief and the vengeance he had planned.

"I'll get them, Blackie," he said to himself with heaving chest. "I know who they are and I'm gonna bomb out the whole Estrada Court until I kill every one of the bastards."

I recognized the reference to Estrada Courts as pertaining to the housing project which is the focus of VNE (*Varria Nueva Estrada*) gang activity.

"It won't do any good to continue the killing," I said. "You'll just get yourself killed, too."

"I don't care; those *putos* deserve it."

I couldn't expect Filas to feel Christian forgiveness in these hours of fresh agony. Even those who have practiced it in small things all their lives have a hard time eliciting it in times of crisis. All I could hope for was that grief would not lead to action for a while. He ranted on: "The cops had one of those fucking *putos*, but you know what they did, Brother?"

"No."

"They turned him loose—lack of evidence. I've got the evidence." He raised one monstrous arm. "Right here in my fist." And he smashed it furiously into the cushioned seat of the sofa.

"Easy. Take it easy," I said. "Let me take you home."

"By God, by my mother, by the Church, I swear I'll kill those mother fuckers." These were not ordinary angry threats. They were wrenched from deep down. I couldn't fight with fumes and passion.

"I'll get the car key," I said.

On the way to his house he lapsed into silence. I dared not whisper the "Our Father" with its "forgive as we forgive," for fear that Filas would ridicule it. Later he might remember having done so and make it a pattern for his life. I gently tried a "Hail Mary" and its "hour of death." He made no comment, just staggered out of the car to his house.

As I drove home I thought how ironic it is that one of the favorite brands of paint for Filas' and Blackie's "highs" is called "Life."

Photo 7 - Car Wash

5 BLACKIE AND FRANKIE

On the following evening all of my younger *cholos y cholas* who had known Blackie and were good friends to Filas, came to ask me to have a "religion meeting" even though there was none scheduled. I took them into the class-room, led a few prayers, and arranged to take them all to the wake and to the funeral. They also wanted to have another carwash to make money for some flowers for Blackie.

After the meeting, when we stepped outside, there was a big guy, about eighteen years old, sitting on one of the schoolyard benches. He was hunched over in a dark corner. Hopie went over to him for a minute, then came back to me. He said, "That's Big Frankie, best friend of Blackie; he wants to talk to you."

When we had shaken hands, he put his arm around my shoulder saying, "Can we go for a walk, Brother, away from these kids?"

We started walking slowly and he said, "I want to tell you about Blackie. You know me and him was best friends."

I mumbled an acknowledgement.

"We had a couple of good things going, Blackie and me. We used to have drinking contests to see who could kill the most quarts. I gotta admit that was fun. We'd each buy about five quarts and then he'd start drinking—and drink until he couldn't hold any more. Then I started and when I'd had as much as I could hold, we totaled up the score. Blackie usually won."

"How'd you get to be such good buddies?"

"I got into the Valley about three years ago. Some other guys jumped me in with hits and kicks, but he didn't believe it."

I had heard of "jumping in" before. It's the name for the gang initiation process.

By this time we had strolled out of the school-yard and were walking along the street. Remembering the story of the soldier killed while walking with his gang friend, I watched passing cars anxiously. There might be a gun pointing in my direction!

"Anyway," Big Frankie continued, "since Blackie didn't believe me, I had him jump me in personally. From then on we were the best of buddies."

I became apprehensive. We were moving deeper into Li'l Valley territory. The street turned and started down a steep hill—into the Valley. I wanted to stop, but I treasured this rare communication.

Big Frankie flowed on. "One time Blackie decided he wouldn't get drunk anymore. So he took some pills to make him throw up if he did any drinking. But then he saw what fun we were having at a party so he forced it down. When we were almost all collapsed around the room and I had taken off my shoes, he couldn't hold it any longer. He threw up all over my shoes just when my girlfriend was bending over to pick them up. Well, you know, because I was drunk, I kicked her and she fell right in the throw-up!"

Frankie had to laugh at that. "Hey, we're near my house," he said, "come on in and let me tell you more about Blackie.

He was messing up pretty bad just before his death. He broke into a lady's house two blocks away and hit her with a brick.

"He didn't hit her very hard so she lived to testify and he got four months. When he got out, he was trying to go straight when they killed him."

That last turn of phrase, in such good English, made me think of this young man as the intelligent, well-educated fellow which his handsome and well-groomed appearance had hinted at before he opened his mouth and revealed the reality.

"Do you mean you think he was killed by accident?"

"Well, Brother, you know how it is; there doesn't really need to be much of a reason for one gang to go gunning for another. Maybe someone saw him X-ing out a VNE gang name or saw him dragging through VNE territory and decided to finish him off. But, like I say, he'd been in stir for a while and had hardly been out long enough for anyone to know he was out. Maybe it was just a case of mistaken identity."

"How come you got into the gang?" I asked as he plugged in an iron and started laying out a pair of brown khaki flares on the ironing board.

"I don't know; everybody else was in. Ah, those were the good ol' days, Brother. We used to drink awhile, then go cruising the *varrio* or the boulevard, talking to all the chicks. You know, Brother, some people won't believe this, but I had a sort of feeling about Blackie's death about a week and a half before it happened.

"I was going to bed one night, lying right here on the bed where you sit now, and I saw a kind of shadow. Then I heard Blackie saying, 'Hey, Frankie-boy!' He used to call me Frankie-boy. So I said, 'Sit down.' 'Can't stay. Can't stay,' came the reply. So I got up to get him to sit down—and he just disappeared. It gave me a real funny feeling. Now I know why."

He meticulously ironed the pair of pants. "You sure do a careful job on these," I said.

"O, yeah, they gotta be just right. The old lady doesn't understand, and if you send them to the cleaners, they crease them just the opposite of what we want."

"You mean they're part of the gang uniform?"

"Oh sure, Brother; haven't you noticed everyone wears them, either brown or blue or gray?"

"Yeah, but I thought it was just by accident."

"Nope."

His brother came in. He'd recently returned from the service. I asked if he'd been drafted and he said, "Nah, the judge told me to sign for four years or he'd give me two years in jail for gang activity and assault with a deadly weapon." We chatted a while longer, then I left, agreeing to meet him at Blackie's wake.

The wake was to be held at a nearby funeral home. Usually a priest says the Rosary in the presence of the people who have come to view the remains. I thought it would be appreciated by Filas if I could arrange to take part in the ceremonies.

Father Emrick and I teamed up not only to alternate decades of the Rosary, but to give a reading. The casket was at the front of a long narrow room and was separated from the major portion of the room by a railing. Father Emrick and I knelt at the railing with our backs to the crowd of about 150 which was enough to overflow the pews and spill out the door.

Since the number in the crowd set a new record for my association with gang-related people, as I knelt with my back to the crowd, I decided I had better prepare myself psychologically for death at any moment.

Later, when I mentioned my state of mind to Hopie, he thought he was being reassuring to me by telling me that if any rival gangsters had showed up, the Li'l Valley people would have recognized them. I thought, "Yeah, and they would have had a shoot-out right there behind my back!"

The crowd wasn't very responsive to the prayers. Many of them were probably like one of the girls of my gang: although she was fourteen years old and called herself Catholic, she didn't even know the Lord's Prayer.

I gave a reading after the third decade of the Rosary. The text referred to Lazarus rising from the grave and it elicited various sighs, groans, sobs, and even grunts of approval from the people. These reminded me of the *amen*'s I had heard at Baptist services, but they are unusual at a Catholic service.

When we had finished, Father Emrick and I started to leave by passing down the aisle through the crowd. There were sobs audible from different locations, but the most striking, even scary, occurrence was when a man of about thirty arose ominously from the third row and split the silence with, "Father." Father Emrick turned toward him and another eruption came, "Father, I want to confess myself."

It was obvious to everyone that he wanted to be more ready for death than Blackie had been. The reality of the nearness of death was forced upon all of us. Somewhat astounded by the unusual request, Father Emrick's mental shift of gears showed on his face, but he managed to make the transition and disappeared with the man up some stairs to a private room.

I stepped out into the street. As I emerged people were scurrying for cover amid the parked cars and around the corners of buildings. I asked what had happened and the reply was that there had been gunfire from down the street. Just then there was a distant sound of gunshot and the first bullet I had ever heard "whished" through the air perhaps 30 feet above our heads. I sprang for the cover of a building and it was five minutes before I ventured forth to take my gang members home.

So many kids had come to the Rosary that I had to make two trips. Hopie and Fernando waited for the second load since they wanted me to drive past the scene of the murder.

As we went by and spray paint was mentioned by someone, Hopie said, "That's what sniffing gets you into."

I was surprised because I thought he probably did it too, but he denied it saying, "It messes up your brain. Look what it's done to Filas." That tickled me since Hopie's such a "tough", but I said nothing and he went on to say, "I don't smoke or drink either. I used to smoke, but I gave it up because it's bad for you." Hopie was only 14 but he had already tried everything.

Photo 8 - Hopie at Age 15

6 HELPING THE KIDS

The next Sunday, on our church steps, I met a beautiful young woman in her early twenties. She was Maria Elena Amparan, elder sister of one of the Li'l Valley gang members, and she was organizing a meeting of gangs with representatives of the news media in an attempt to make the hazards of East LA gang life known to authorities who might be able to stop the killings.

Maria's meeting was to be held at a nearby school at 7 PM. I gathered my kids and walked them to the meeting. There were lots of TV lights and cameras set up and a few adults sitting inside when the appointed hour arrived. The kids were showing their usual aversion for anything authoritative and organized. Only a few of them would sign their names as they were requested to do at the door and they then turned around and walked out.

I guess Maria was expecting more people to come, for she kept waiting to start. Meanwhile the kids were stacking up on the school steps and getting more and more restless. As I had warned Maria, violence broke out. I was inside at the time, reading the press release about Blackie's death. Suddenly everyone who had filtered part of the way into the meeting room rushed outside. Kids have a funny way of "not knowing" what happened whenever something happens. All I know is that when I got outside, people were whispering about Filas. I understood that someone had thrown a bottle either from or at a passing car and that Filas and some other dudes had chased the car on foot. They were dimly visible halfway down the block. When someone said that the people in the car had a gun many of us moved quickly out of the doorway.

By now it was 7:30 and Maria still was not convinced that she should get the meeting started. Instead, she just wandered around talking to reporter Harold Greene of Channel 7, several radio men, the police chief, and some other city and county officials. She finally started at 7:45.

After a brief emotion-filled statement during which she almost broke into tears and in which she wondered when the Mexican people would stop killing themselves off, she threw the meeting open to statements from the audience.

First, she asked for some of the gang members to say something. I tried to get one of my boys named Roki to tell about our attempts to get out of the streets by having carwashes and planning trips. None of the kids would speak, but they encouraged me to take the microphone.

I rose and said I had been trying to do something practical to move the kids out of the streets, but that after we had earned enough money, the community center, which had promised us a bus, kept holding out on us. I said we needed some concrete help in the form of transportation.

I have never before or since made a speech which roused so much reaction. I had not been back in my seat for 30 seconds when a man tapped me on the shoulder and motioned me to the rear of the room for a talk.

He introduced himself as the head of the community center and was very upset that I had indicated that his center was either going back on its word or was inadequate to help in my efforts. He introduced me to Gene Tanaka who was at that time a Deputy Probation Officer of LA County, and together they insisted that I take the floor again and retract my implication that the center wasn't doing its job.

They promised me that, if the bus wasn't working or the driver was ailing, I would be given either vans by the community center or county cars by the probation department. That sounded good to me so I made a clarification.

When the meeting broke up, I was swamped by people: mothers of older gang members who said they would help me keep my younger crew off the streets; 25-ish guys who apparently had outgrown a gang and were offering their own cars and vans to help me take the boys to the snow; other adults with less practical transportation suggestions. Of all the people who had spoken, I was the only one who was on the scene and doing something concrete with a group of youngsters.

By eleven that evening I was relaxing with the TV News. It showed Maria as she spoke and then gave a statement from one of the older gang members. The camera panned over the crowd and even showed my clan so I know the day is preserved in the news files of LA's Channel 7. It was February 7, 1973.

The death of Blackie was having a few side benefits!

7 TRIAL TRIP

The following Sunday I had the snow trip ready to go for the whole crew and on the previous day I used my day off to take a carload of boys for what turned out to be quite an outing. I still didn't know the individual youngsters very well, so I just told Hopie, who was always bugging me to take them somewhere, to gather a carload.

It was raining in LA, so I promised myself I would go far enough to find some fine weather for the boys. But, as we drove along with the windows rolled up, *my* day was nothing but miserable.

The boys' favorite food (sometimes I had the impression it was their only food) was sunflower seeds which they referred to as "poly-seeds." They had a big bagful and insisted that they were so hungry they had to eat them even though the stench as they cracked the seeds with their teeth and talked at the same time was making me sick.

To make things worse, as we traveled the freeways, slick with months of accumulated oil droppings, the boys in the back seat felt like having a fight with the ones in the front.

The car literally rocked with merriment before I could tame them down.

I noticed that one boy, Efren, the one who might pass for the twin of either his brother Fernando or of their friend Hopie, did a lot of participating (slugging and pushing) and smiled broadly but never said a word. So I tried to get to know him by means of various questions, all of which were answered adeptly by someone else before he could speak.

Finally I demanded that they let him speak for himself. Then the truth came out. "He never speaks," the others told me. He can do so, they say, but does it so rarely that most members of the gang have never heard him. I was alarmed, but dropped the subject for fear of embarrassing him.

We were driving north, headed in the general direction of a mountainous park called "The Devil's Punchbowl." We got around the mountains and outran the rain as we stopped at Vista Point overlooking the Antelope Valley

Suddenly the wind blew off Efren's hat. Without uttering a sound, he plunged down a formidable precipice to retrieve it. Before it could even enter my mind as possible, the other boys were gone too!

Once they reached the plain below, they kept on going. They hopped a fence and started throwing rocks and dirt clods into the California Aqueduct which carries water from Northern California to LA. I am sure their barrage was illegal. I might have shouted to them, but they were too far away by then and would not have heeded me anyway.

Hopie spotted a pipe crossing the approximately 30-foot channel and walked briskly across it. The pipe's diameter was about one foot and it scared me just to *think* of walking it about 15 feet above a channel of water of unknown depth. Besides that, the bed of the channel was made of concrete.

Another guy started to follow Hopie as I stood riveted 500 yards away, hopeless either to stop them or to rescue them should someone fall into the water. I felt better when that boy got as far as a big coupling on the pipe, found it fearsome, and turned back, straddling the pipe and hanging on with legs and arms as he crawled back to safety.

Hopie started a war of rocks across the water so Fernando went to join him with a similar brisk and daring walk across the pipe. Others soon lined up to try the walk, but chickened out.

I calmed myself. It wouldn't do any good to watch, so I studied the map of the region, looked for educational tidbits which might interest the gang, and I scanned the horizon for the San Andreas Fault which was supposedly ahead of us on our road. Then I picked up some aluminum cans while waiting for the kids to return.

They all made it back safely about 20 minutes later. We set out to cross the San Andreas Fault. It came at a slight rise in the road and the rock formations where the road had been cut through indicated something of the great contortions which the earth has gone through at various times.

The sedimentary layers were generally wavy, but showed a marked slanting outward from both sides of the center. To my surprise, the kids did not seem at all interested in the source of LA's earthquakes. My explanations scarcely brought a sound from them.

They responded with only slightly more enthusiasm when I asked what they thought about the word "Chicano." A discussion had arisen in the rectory about the meaning of the word and it had been determined that neither native Mexicans of high estate nor Mexican-Americans who are well established in America like the word unless they are active in political movements like the Chicano Liberation Front. So I said, "What do you guys think about the word 'Chicano'; do you like it?"

Hopie, with his usual calm reply said, "It's alright."

"Would you be willing to let someone call you a Chicano?"

"Sure. That's what we are."

"Do you know anyone who wouldn't like to be called that?"

It was Fernando who answered, "No. Not no one."

"Not no one?" I said, "What kind of English is that?"

"It's the way we speak," came from Li'l James who is at least a year older than the others.

"But do you know the correct way to say it Fernando?"

"Sure."

"What is it?"

"Not *anyone*." He said saucily.

This was the only time "Chicano" was ever mentioned in all my dealings with the Los Homes Gang.

I did not really know where to turn off for "The Devil's Punch Bowl" so I kept going to Palmdale where we stopped for food and directions. I bought a special child's plate for each. They did not tear the place up very much, though their manners were atrocious.

Fernando kept asking me in a whisper if I would like to buy some 50¢ "reds" from him. They are a variety of dope so I answered that I might, thinking I could use them as evidence against him if I turned him in to the police. But I did not really want to turn him in if there were any other way to help him out of such bad business.

We had to backtrack a bit, but at last found "The Devil's Punch Bowl" high up in the foothills and only about five miles from St. Andrew's Priory at a town called Valyermo. I had been wanting to visit the Benedictine monastery there. Rain was falling when we got to the Punch Bowl. Ours was the only car in the parking lot. I had not come all this way to be turned back by a little rain so we went hiking to get some idea of the formations.

The rocks were tremendous (larger than houses)! They looked like rounded boulders, yet were mostly juttings-out of rock formations still buried deep in the earth. Strangest of all was the composition of the rocks, not smooth and homogeneous like most boulders, but rough like coarse

Photo 9- Pre-trip Checkup

sandpaper and composed of the fusing together of sand and pebbles.

As soon as the boys had realized the vastness of the rock formations and how they formed many crevices for exploration, each went a different direction to investigate.

From up close these out-croppings are not pretty; they are of the consistency and ugliness of man-made concrete. They would have been great for climbing, except that a cold drizzle was lashed over our bodies by a wind whirling off the overhanging mountains.

The scrambling kids seemed oblivious to the cold, but I realized that we would soon be hopelessly separated from each other if I did not call them back. We returned to the car and went on to St. Andrew's.

The rain stopped. Massive cottonwood trees lined the short approach to the Priory over a dirt road. At this time of year those mammoth trees looked gloomily stark as their leafless branches speared the sky.

The boys were silent and I feared they would not like the place. Visible through the trees was a white wooden building of ancient ranch style.

A robed monk with his head in some reading material was slowly moving towards another building and did not look up until we forced his attention by driving up beside him. He was Brother Paul, about 20 years old and very handsome.

He was willing to show us around even though a sign we had seen on a curio shop said it was closed. But the boys were not out of the car two minutes before they hopped a pasture fence and were chasing half-a-dozen sheep and demanding rides of them!

Brother and I stood there watching, to be sure the boys did not run the sheep to death. They were very fat animals and I wondered if fat old animals have heart attacks.

Once the boys caught and straddled them, they would not budge, so the crew turned to a penned cow. Her pen was about 25 feet square. That kept her well enough enclosed for

Hopie and the others to catch her and also gave her enough room to give them a nice ride, or so they thought.

She had other ideas. She either shook them off or rubbed them off against the side of the pen, an operation which could be very dangerous. When Efren became her victim, it looked like he might at last say something, but he remained mute while he limped away from the game.

The boys now spotted a group of ponies about 500 yards away across a field of desert sand. Brother Paul and I followed the resultant stampede of human hooves.

As we walked, he told me that these ponies had once belonged to Disneyland, but were here at the monastery because they had proven too wild to be ridden. We could see from a distance that the boys were already discovering that. The ponies would not stand still long enough for the boys to mount them and a few nips from their big teeth were enough to discourage any further efforts at closeness.

As a less dangerous and more educational pursuit, I suggested a hike in the nearby foothills. I even moved off into the Joshua trees (cacti about 20 feet high with branches reminiscent of ordinary trees but totally covered with yucca-like spiny leaves), hoping they would follow me. I nosed among the interesting rocks and became familiar with Juniper bushes which seemed to be a sort of scraggly evergreen similar to a cedar. But the boys could not be budged from their fascination with the untouchable ponies!

Brother Paul arranged for us to have supper with the monks after Vespers. Monastic tradition jokingly says, "You don't pray, you don't eat." If we wanted to eat, we figured we had better stay with him.

We herded my flock into the last row of the chapel, a small building in the shape of a cross with the limbs of the cross so fat that the feel for the design, I am sure, escaped my boys. In the arms of the cross, there were seats for 40 monks. We sat in the nave with about 20 other visitors.

Each of us was given a binder notebook containing the prayers in English. Mistletoe, which Hopie had found on a tree in the yard, received more attention than the Psalms of Vespers. That trial past, we moved to another building to dine.

In a sort of waiting room, we had to rub shoulders with monks and the other groups of people who had been at Vespers. I was afraid this society would be the most severe test of all for my boys. Luckily, they spied a chess board and started to play. Alfred, somewhat older than the others, seemed to be the instructor.

We had a table to ourselves in the refectory, but there was only salad on it. Hopie asked in a whisper, "Is this all we get, Brother?" But soon trays of baked chicken, stewed cabbage, and profusely-buttered mashed potatoes were set on a table in mid-room.

As people finished their salads, they went to serve themselves. When the boys understood the system they went wild, in a hushed sort of way, stacking their plates high, emptying them, and going back for more even though we had eaten less than three hours earlier.

Brother Paul enjoyed my unusual friends and asked Brother Anthony over to join us. When it was over, the Brothers invited us to return sometime. The boys showed their appreciation by taking fistfuls of homemade bread with them when we left the table!

We drove home happily in the worsening rain. I could not have dared hope for such a good response from my gang. Not only did they not turn up their noses at the idea of having visited a monastery: they begged me to take them again the next Saturday!

8 SNOW JOKE

Whoever wrote the song, "It Never Rains in Southern California," certainly must have written it in the fall of the year, toward the end of the annual 10-month drought. During December and January, rain is frequent and when it rains in LA, it snows in the mountains.

Of all the people who had promised me vans and cars, only two showed up, but that was enough. I crammed those vans full of kids and managed to convince Father Nolan to let me use a parish car for the remaining trippers.

One of the vans was a huge, brand-spanking-new shiny purple thing with carpeted interior. It was owned by a 20-ish member of the Li'l Valley Gang, a *veterano*, one who was slowly phasing out his gang activity by holding down a job and becoming active in a car club with his fancy van. All of the kids wanted to ride in there, especially as I learned later, the ones who wanted to sniff paint all the way to the snow and back!

The other van was owned and driven by Clete, a college boy whom I had met as a result of my tennis teaching. He considered himself to be "deeply into Jesus" and so wanted to

Photo 10 - Typical *Cholas*

help me with my youth work, at least this once. Poor Clete! If he had realized how inimical these kids are to this kind religion, he might not have been so willing. This trip was to be a more novel experience for him than it was for the natives of East LA!

Because part of the transportation was being furnished by a Li'l Valley *veterano*, he brought two other LV members with him, one from the division called The Dukes and another from The Santos (Saints). So I had a 17-year-old, 210-pound, football player suggesting that he ride along in my car. I had a feeling I had better be gracious. Also in my car was a beautiful girl named Star, 15, and her two professed bodyguards, one of them replete with caked-on makeup and with the icy, jaded eyes of an old pro.

Star was so beautiful that some of the guys said she could steal almost any girl's boyfriend at will. All the girls disliked her and this was especially true of *La* Rosie.

Rosie had threatened to kill Star and Star had no reason to think this was a bluff. In fact, when Rosie had been helping me phone people to tell particulars about the trip, she had written me a note at the bottom of the page of names. It said, "Star *can't come* unless you want her to come back in *ice*!"

It was due to this threat on her life that Star and her friends were riding in my car. We first went up the road toward Crystal Lake, but a police car was parked in the middle of a bridge just below the mountains. Over the car's loudspeaker we heard that the road ahead was closed, due to mud slides. I got out and asked the officer if he knew the condition of the road to Mount Baldy. He told us to call the Pomona Highway Patrol.

The nearest business establishment was a sad-looking barroom populated by people who looked as left-over from the night before as the smoke in the room. I did not hesitate to go in to use the phone, but I could feel Clete cringing at my side.

When the kids all decided they needed to use the restrooms, they were inside before I even saw them coming. The proprietors may have been alarmed at the under-age raid, but they realized how futile protest would be, so they simply watched.

The Pomona Highway Patrol answered with a recording which said nothing at all about Baldy, but we went anyway. Clete was starting to hesitate at the prospect of adding further to our long drive only to be turned back again, but he reluctantly followed in line.

I knew Baldy to be the most accessible mountain I had ever seen. There are scarcely any hairpin curves on the road and not even many hills. You just follow your nose in the general direction for about five miles after the houses quit, and suddenly you have a rather difficult incline. Go through two tunnels which look like they have been used for several movies and probably have, top a rise, and dip back into a little valley.

The valley had a light covering of snow. The kids broke into cheers. Judging by that valley and the cars coming down from the mountains stacked with snowballs, we knew we were going to make it.

Another mile further and we came to several small stores and some commercial trout fishing pools. The snow was a foot deep and the road got narrower. Just then we saw a sign: "Proceed No Further Without Chains." Typical California highway department efficiency, I thought, always there with the right sign at the right moment. We got one of the last possible safe parking spots. A suddenly-thick stream of cars behind us was getting into trouble: a road full of foot-deep snow.

Usually when kids from LA visit the mountains, they find snow which may have been there for weeks. It is packed hard as ice and full of dirt. This time some snow still clung to the boughs of the trees in spite of a persistent light rain.

It was beautiful, but under foot was pure misery. The rain on the snow made a slush that none of us had properly prepared for. But the kids did not utter a single complaint. Certainly it was because they did not know any better since they had never experienced snow in its more comfortable textures. They waded off in the direction of a sliding slope while Clete and I waited in line at the hamburger stand.

Since our transportation had not cost us the money we had made washing cars, we would spend it on food. The burgers cost 70 cents each, about twice what we would expect to pay in LA at that time, but we were glad to have food at any price.

By that time Clete had begun to know my Crew. "Hilary," he said, "I'm not so sure there's any hope for these kids. I ask them to be careful of the cabinet in my van but they kept kicking it and sitting on it.

"Well, Clete, old buddy," I said, "You just gotta be patient."

"Yeah, but when I asked them to please be more considerate, they said, 'What's that the funny paddy say?' A while later when they were quieter, I asked them if they knew Jesus and they said, 'Is he a pussy like you?' Then they joked around saying, 'Claass! Claa-aaass! Let's all be sure to go to Sunday school this week; you all want to be saved do you not?' Some others answered, 'Aw, shut up, you fucking *gringa puta* and quit givin' us that shitty grin'."

I had to laugh. But I assured him they would not usually be so blasphemous except when someone gets too pushy with religion.

Fun as the snow was, we had not been there more than an hour-and-a-half when the kids became so wet and cold and tired of the snow that most of them were curled up in the purple van's shag carpeting, sniffing their paint fumes. It was time to leave.

Once we got out of the mountains we could see the sky clearing from the West. In the clean, fresh air, East LA looked well. But trouble was brewing among the kids when we got back.

The vans had preceded me and dropped them in the schoolyard. One of the Li'l Valley gangmen had stuck Irene in the van on the way home. She was now in the restroom of the rectory, crying and re-arranging her make-up.

I asked the boys what had happened and they said Hopie had been "trying a little *manos-manos*," meaning, as they showed me by sign, exploration of her upper anatomy. She had shooed him away and was looking the other way when someone else tried it. She thought it was Hopie again and kicked him in the face as they were all seated on the van floor. That made him slug her a few times.

That ended our great snow trip. I never saw Clete again.

Photo 11 - Inspirational Gang Mural

9 GOIN' FISHIN'

From then on, Hopie knew he could get a trip out of me at least once a week if he pestered me enough. And he did. He and Fernando would come to the rectory and ask the secretary to call me out. It got to be such a constant thing that the secretaries would simply say, "Your little friends are here."

Sometimes as many as half-a-dozen of the kids would come into the rectory at the same time. A half dozen ordinary boys are not noted for being silent, but these guys would ring the bell at least five times, kick the door, shove one another into the seats provided for visitors, and slap their hands on the high desk demanding, "We wanna see Brother Hilary!" The desk was long and high so it protected the secretary from the boys, but no matter which secretary was on duty they were a worry. She would quickly phone my room and say, "Would you please come down here to tame your friends?"

Father Nolan got tired of these invasions and instructed me to tell the boys to wait for me outside. I never was very successful in convincing them. They knew they would get faster action if they riled a few people.

One time when I was chatting with Hopie and the crew, I made the mistake of telling them about the grunion. The grunion is a fish of the smelt family, about ten inches long, which at full moon and high tide, rides the surf onto the beach, burrows into the sand to lay its eggs, and then flops back toward the water. People are allowed to catch them at certain times of the year, but the elusive grunion usually manages to break pattern often enough to discourage his hunters.

In other words, when most people have been reading the moon and tide charts and are waiting with buckets to catch some grunion, the fish do not appear. On the other hand, when a cool or cloudy evening keeps people in their homes, the grunion sometimes "run" in such numbers that the beach becomes coated with flopping, silvery fish and looks like a long, flowing, sequined gown.

One such night, I told the boys, I happened to be nearly alone on Santa Monica Pier. When I glanced over the guard rail, my heart started to pound. Was this the fabled grunion run my grandfather had described to me so many years ago when I had visited him in San Diego?

I looked again to be sure this was not just the glint of water on sand. Then I broke into a frenzied run, frantically looking in trash cans for some box or can to put grunion in. Soon I was the only person on the beach, alone with perhaps 10,000 grunion! It was one of the most exciting experiences of my life.

My dad had often taken me fishing in Oklahoma and Colorado and even on the piers of California, but a good case of frustration was about all I ever caught. An occasion like this was true therapy for such years of thwarted desire. With my bare hands I grabbed the barbless fish, scooping up a handful of sand to improve my grip on the slippery things.

I might have gotten hundreds of pounds of fish if the physical exertion and the excitement of my heart had not worn me down. Besides that, I did not want to take more than I could use so I quit with about 50. Still it was hard for me to tear myself away. I had come to know something of the tug of "gold fever," that craving which makes a man hoard more and more of a commodity when he realizes he is surpassing his ability to carry it all away.

Grunion hunting can be done totally on the sand so I might have left the beach without ever getting my good shoes wet except for one particularly greedy moment when I scooped too long for a fish even though I saw a new wave approaching.

If the story above has not awoken an itch in my reader, it certainly did so in the souls of my youngsters one evening when I was trying particularly hard to interest them in something I might do for them. They never forgot about grunion. For the next several months I would never be allowed to overlook a full moon. They would warn me days in advance, "Brother Hilary, it's going to be full moon next Saturday."

That meant I had to load up the car with kids and buckets and once again describe all the minutiae of grunion stalking while we made the 20-mile beeline down the Santa Monica Freeway. Unfortunately, at least the first few times, it began to seem to the kids that Brother Hilary was no more reliable than any of the other adults they had dealt with.

When we found no grunion and I had to get home by a reasonable hour, it was construed as an indication that I really did not care if they had any fun. As I dropped them at their homes one night, rather than thanking me for my time and effort, they stood in the street shouting after me, "*Cholo*," a term of many interpretations, this time seemingly used with derogation. (But at least by calling me *cholo* they had put me in a category somewhat more acceptable to them than "T.J.," which refers to anyone who has just come over the border, or paddy or Anglo, terms used for any white man whose ways they cannot stomach.)

Since I had failed to produce grunion, they obliged me to take them pier fishing every so often. Though I could not bear to participate in such a boring sport, I arranged to take them to Redondo or Manhattan Beach.

I usually explored seaside shops while the kids fished, but on one memorable occasion I managed to make friends with Fernando by taking him sight-seeing when his fishing gear broke. Together we studied the operation of an oil drilling rig and poked our heads into the cabin cruisers at Marina Del Ray, supposedly the world's largest man-made marina. Fancy fishing poles and tiny TV sets aboard the boats caught Fernando's eye so I had occasion to mention the commandment, "Thou shall not steal."

Now that I had Fernando alone, I wanted to ask him what he had meant by calling me *cholo* that night of our grunion hunt. I had asked several people in and around the rectory since that night and had received such conflicting meanings that I had decided the important thing was what Ferny had meant when he used the term.

One lady, for example, who had grown up in a gang of the *pachuco* era said that "the *pachuco* of yesteryear is the *cholo* of today." I concluded that she meant to define a *cholo* as a "gang member."

When I had asked Hopie its meaning saying, "Does it mean like 'wetback?' " he replied, "Na-uh. It's a bad word. I don't know how you say it."

"Well," I said, "are you willing to let someone call you a *cholo?*"

"Yeah."

Some girls had told me the term "stone *cholo*" meant a real dyed-in-the-wool *cholo*: khakis, sandals, hair combed back, wearing a bandana sweat band, standing with legs together and toes turned outward, and slugging his arms back with chin up. They added that a *chola* (female of the species), is characterized by "white sandals, creased levis, halter top, three pairs of false eyelashes, and white eyeshadow."

After all this I was very interested in exactly what Fernando had meant when he had called me a *cholo*. I certainly did not dress like that and I was not a gang member. He said, "Aw, it don't mean nothing bad. You were wearing those khakis that night."

"You mean this pair of dark blue, flared levis?"

"Yeah, thems are khakis."

"But lots of people wear these. What makes someone be a *cholo*?"

"It's like when you go out late on the streets like we do; you know how we do. And it was about ten o'clock when you brought us home that night so I called you a *cholo*."

My only possible conclusion was that he had applied the word *cholo* to me in a very loose sense. More strictly, judging by the consensus of the people I talked to, the term *cholo* would refer to, as one lady said, "more a manner of dressing and acting than to gang membership." It seems to me that the term *cholo* is most frequently used to encompass anyone who is either a gang member or a gang sympathizer (one who has gang friends) and who is dressed in "gang uniform". I was soon to learn the importance of these distinctions.

10 FRONT SEAT SHOTGUN

The general esteem for the game of tennis in East LA was very low when I arrived. I never tried to push my favorite sport on the boys lest they label it as "sissy." But when my relationship had advanced to such a point that they were following my every move, it was just a matter of time before they would try the game.

I was spending my Saturday mornings teaching tennis for the Park Department of the neighboring affluent City of Montebello. One Saturday when I told the boys I could not take them anywhere until after I had finished teaching, two of the older one, Alfred and Li'l James, decided to accompany me.

I had always expected they would be good at the game because they had to be good athletes and well-coordinated to survive so well in the streets and alleyways of East L.A. I was right. They took up some rackets and proceeded to give a close fight in their very first set to two ladies I was training. They were on their way to being hooked on tennis!

On the afternoon of their first match I took them to the Los Angeles Harbor tourist attraction called Ports o' Call. It

Photo 12 - Front Seat Shotgun

is modeled like an old time fishing village, but all the houses are full of trinkets for sale. When I stopped to investigate various starfish and cowrie shells in a shop called The Mermaid's Dowry, my boys kept on moving.

By the time I had caught up to them, they were on their bellies on a sidewalk, offering a new tourist attraction. A certain restaurant had a sort of moat around it filled with water and goldfish. Beside the moat was a sidewalk which meandered around and eventually crossed over the moat.

There the boys were, flat on their stomachs on the bridge, forcing people to step over them while they dangled their arms into the water making vain stabs at the fish. I figured it was about the most fun and least expensive or bothersome thing they could do so I let them continue.

That this outing was not the ordinary Saturday afternoon family affair where the kids take a trip with daddy was made more obvious as we started piling into the car for departure. Hopie had gotten to the Ports o' Call by riding "front seat shotgun," i.e., next to the window in the front seat. It was only reasonable that someone else should be allowed that most favored of all positions on the trip home.

As I unlocked the car, the boys shouldered each other at the doors, jockeying for the chance to be either on my side of the car as I opened my door or on the other side begging me to toss them the key so they could unlock the door and get in first. Somehow Alfred and Efren got the two front seats. Hopie would not allow that. He refused to get into the car at all if he did not get "front seat shotgun."

I tried pleading with him to recognize the right of someone else to have the favored seat once in a while. I begged him to get into the car. Finally I got out of the car and decided I would force him in.

He was only fourteen years old on the day in question, but if I did not know the strength of a piece of coiled iron such as might be used for springs on a truck, I was about to have a demonstration. Not a speck of fat did the lithe frame of

59

Hopie bear and trying to wrestle him into that car was like trying the same trick with a wild 150-pound baby bull.

He probably did not weigh more than 100 pounds, but his slightness of size just made him harder to hold. There we were, having what must have looked to a passerby like a father-son battle royal in the roadway at the main entrance to Ports o' Call. I had not expected any big struggle, but soon I found my glasses falling off and I was having a problem staying on my feet. When I pushed him toward the open car door, rather than go in, he would poke out an arm and slam it shut.

The battle waged inconclusively for perhaps three full minutes. I was not going to give in. I would regroup my strengths, change my psychological attitude by recognizing that this was no ordinary half-pint foe, set my glasses carefully aside, and methodically dispose of this problem. This had become a matter of honor. How could I let this little punk dictate to me what he would do in my car on my day off when I had taken my time to entertain him?

Then, more suddenly and silently than any lesson I can recall ever having learned before or since, I received an essential lesson in gang leadership. Without saying a word, first Efren and then Alfred got out of the front seat of the car and moved to get into the rear seat. They would not retreat. They said, "Let him slide, Brother. We know Hopie. He won't change his mind. He won't get in and if you put him in, he'll just get out again."

I knew then that Hopie was the leader of the gang. He was the smallest, but he was the most strong-willed. Rather than see me continue to push Hopie around, the rest of the gang was willing to acknowledge his ascendency in a more public way than they had ever done before.

Street life required each boy to be strong in support of his personal rights whether those rights happened to be ones recognized by the rest of society or not, but in this situation they were willing to ignore their personal rights both for the common good and out of deference to their leader. These boys were not just individuals. They did not exist apart from each other. This incident helped join them closer.

The gang, at least in its nucleus, was a society unlike any I had ever experienced before. Its leader was one who had refused to put the common good before his own desires. Yet he was accepted not only as a member of the society, but as the leader. On no level of society had I ever seen such a thing.

The U.S. President and all other government officials must swear to uphold the common good. If they utterly refuse to do so, like Hopie did, they not only are not chosen as leaders, they are ostracized, perhaps even put in jail. Such is also the case on other levels of society: school, church, monastery, and family. Even in societies I have not experienced, such as monarchies, the ruler must look after the common good or face an uprising.

Had I really understood the gang structure properly? Perhaps this was simply a case in which the gang was giving me the ultimate, subtle slap in the face by preferring even the greatest intransigence of Hopie to any of my domination.

Was it just an example of gang honor or was it an indication of the sociological structure of this gang and of gangs in general? Perhaps it was a combination of both, but I am inclined to believe that it was mostly the latter. At any rate, from then on I worked on the premise that Hopie was the leader of the gang, leader in a society which accepted tyrannical domination.

Later when I asked members of various gangs how a person comes to be the leader, their response fitted Hopie's situation perfectly: "He's the one who can kick everybody's ass."

11 NOT A NEW GANG?

One night while I was away teaching tennis, some of the girls had a fight at the tiny market across the street from the church. I did not know about it at all until a lady named Henrietta Lopez came to see me several days later about arranging a meeting of my teenagers.

La Rosie finally had had a good tough fight with Star, a fight which included pulling of hair, biting, scratching, and throwing of milk crates which are usually stacked outside that store. Somebody's mother called the police and now Mrs. Lopez was following up for the county probation department to see if such incidents could be avoided in the future.

Some of the girls watching the fight had come to the rectory to get me, but since I was absent, they took Father Emrick to the scene and he stopped the fight. Father Emrick had given my name to Mrs. Lopez and she wanted me to bring the gang to a newly-opened community center for discussion.

In the course of the meeting, which was attended by only about fifteen of my crew and which sorely lacked the presence of Star and Rosie, I learned for the first time that my boys were not part of the Li'l Valley Midgets as I had always supposed they were since they wrote LV on the walls and seemed to respect the LV.

Now I realized that, although they might have written their names and LV, they never put the two together, never wrote for example, "*El* Hopie-VLV" indicating affiliation with *Varrio* Li'l Valley. The reason they gave for not belonging to the Valley was because scarcely any of them lived in the Li'l Valley territory.

In my dealings with the kids I had always steered clear of mention of gangdom for fear that I would stir up a sort of pride which is associated with gang membership. But on this occasion Mr. Gene Tanaka, also with the probation department, asked point blank what gang they belonged to. He must have thought, as I did, that they certainly showed the symptoms of being members of a Peewee division of some gang.

At first they said, "We ain't from nowhere." Then someone said they belonged to a sort of club called the "Homes." Only one week later, the group had evolved into a fully fledged gang with a special gang insignia, -LH- for *Los* Homes and new secret nicknames, all of which began to appear on the walls of the churchyard and with a gang initiation ceremony called "being jumped in."

After this first meeting at the community center, we had a very interesting walk, about four blocks back to the churchyard, the place which they had publicly claimed in the meeting as their hangout. For some reason, unlike in the past, the boys were refusing to have anything to do with the girls.

On the walk to the meeting the boys had taken a completely separate route. On the return trip the boys and girls were taking different sides of the street. They started calling each other names, one of the most vile outbreaks I have ever heard. I could not even begin to tell the full scene, but a few examples of the language will illustrate the level of the exchange, how much prejudice can readily surface, and how it can escalate warfare.

One girl who is a shade darker than anyone else got called "nigger." She countered with the opposite extreme, "you bleached-out bitch." Thus did insignificant differences in skin shading give rise to a gushing-forth of hatred such as I had never seen before. Like bricks in the hand of a skilled bricklayer slapping bricks into place to make a wall where none existed minutes earlier, the words flew back and forth across the street, one insult building on another.

"*Huero,*" as used in East LA, is the Spanish word for "light-colored" or "blonde" and since the Mexicans are proud of their dark skins and black hair, anyone with a tinge of lightness in either skin or hair lies open to that epithet as an insult or as a friendly nickname depending on the context of usage. In this exchange *huero* was heard in the abusive sense along with *puto*, and *puta* for the females.

I went from side to side of the street to try to soothe the warring forces. Far from being successful, I soon found myself caught in a cross fire as empty cans and pop bottles became missiles! Tempers really flared. The result was a more devastating barrage of words.

The ones mentioned already were abandoned in favor of more creative expressions like, "Your mother's a bleached-out whore" or "Your father sleeps drunk in the gutter." There were also many Spanish phrases, the meaning of which I did not know—fortunately for me!

12 YES, A NEW GANG!

Throughout the months in which I had known Hopie, he had mostly watched my tennis from afar, scarcely making a comment. But one day he happened to catch me giving a lesson to a very pretty young woman in the churchyard. (I usually gave my lessons in various parks.) His interest rose suddenly.

He asked me if I got paid for that and I said, "Yes." I never volunteered to tell the amount because for some people in East L.A. it would have sounded like I must be rich while for people of other regions it would have meant: "If that's all you charge, you must be a pretty worthless teacher." But, on this particular occasion Hopie nosed around just as the lady was slipping me a $5 bill.

"Wow," he said, "did she pay you all that just for teaching her tennis?" Now that he knew, he was more interested than ever in this sport which almost no one else in the immediate area cared anything about. The nearest court was ten blocks from the church and that was so neglected that it usually had no net, was strewn with broken beer bottles, and had baseball "bases" drawn all over it.

Where there were girls and money, Hopie was sure to go. The following Saturday he rose at the crack of dawn to accompany me on my trip of several miles to Montebello Park where I was teaching, among others, a cute little Japanese girl just Hopie's age. If the experience did no good to Hopie, it did wonders for the girl.

When he took up a racket, she showed more interest in the lessons than ever before. I gave them a court of their own to hit on and they hit more tennis balls in the allotted time than had ever been seen in that class. Hopie was hooked. He stayed with me through the whole morning and watched carefully as I explained the techniques of the game to other pupils. From then on, he was eager for more tennis, but on his own terms.

Before I had time for any more tennis with the boys, we had a second meeting with Mrs. Lopez and Mr. Tanaka but this time at our church in the parish hall. Father Nolan was reluctant to let us use the hall for fear the kids would mess it up. I assured him I would have the assistance of two trained social workers and that we would watch everything carefully.

La Rosie came to this meeting and was the center of attention. Mrs. Lopez wanted to know the source of the Rosie-Star conflict. "Boys," they said. Would it end? "No." How about a public, adult-supervised wrestling match? Rosie liked that idea, but was sure Star's mother would not allow anything which might endanger the looks of her precious daughter.

When the meeting broke up, I thought the kids would bolt from the hall while I chatted with Mrs. Lopez. Instead, Alfred headed for the stage where he fascinated the younger kids with his ability on the piano. I still do not know where he learned to play.

Too many things started happening so I did not get around to discussing the piano with Alfred. From somewhere there had appeared three little tiny kids about five years old. I had never seen them before. They were very dirty and unruly—obviously the next generation of gang sympathizers.

The dance wax on the stage invited them to have a sliding party. After sliding several feet on their knees, they found themselves enveloped in the stage curtains. The game changed to "Slide and Hide." By the time I had mounted the stage, kids were whirring in every direction, driven on by the tempo of the piano music.

If Father Nolan had come on the scene, I probably would not be here to tell about it. Of course the gang could not understand why all of this should not be allowed. But I could still hear Father Nolan saying, "If they mess up the hall, it'll be the last time you'll ever use it."

I stationed Gene Tanaka at the door to make sure that once a kid went out, he did not come back. I shooed everyone off the stage to the best of my knowledge, but the slide-and-hide game may have left a few bodies lurking in the stage curtains, dark corners, or the various cabinets. When I had satisfied myself that all were out, I went to the restrooms to be sure no one was hiding there.

I had warned the kids that Father Nolan would never let us use this hall again if they wrote on the walls, tables or floor, but in the girl's restroom I found *Los* Homes *Locas* in the very neat gang-style of printing.

Often when I find writing somewhere I am tempted to dismiss it as having been there for weeks, but this had to be fresh tonight for it was at this meeting that the kids announced that since last week's meeting, they had formed the *Los* Homes Gang to "stick up for" each other when any one of them should get in a fight, like Rosie had with Star. This restroom writing indicated that the female division of the gang was calling itself *Las Locas*, Literally, "Female Crazies." Several other gangs had divisions called *Locos* so I was not surprised!

This announcement of the formation of the *Los* Homes Gang was a great blow to me. It seemed as though all the work I had been doing with the kids was moving them in exactly the opposite direction from what I had intended.

Interesting, however, was the sociological change in status. I realized that, until the past week, my crew had been nothing but gang sympathizers, the less organized type of *cholo*. Now I remembered that their graffiti had never before indicated any gang affiliation. I could see that it was one thing to write "*El* Hopie—*Rifa*" and quite another to write "*El* Hopie—R*LH*R."

Readers familiar with the gang scene may be tempted to question the true gang nature of this group in comparison to well-established gangs. I hasten to point out that one could certainly not ask for a more likely start of a new gang, for Hopie was the youngest of six boys and my talks with his father indicated that every one of the five older boys was a member of a *different* well-established gang.

Furthermore, Hopie had been asked to join the *Lomita Primera* gang and had not yet done so only because he was too young to drive and lived too far away. Admittedly, this gang was more akin to the Peewee division of a gang since all of its members were still too young to drive. But even the Peewee division of a gang is very significant to society for obvious reasons.

After thanking the community center people once again for their help and interest, I found all the girls gathered outside on the grass in a small (about 40' x 40') area between rectory and church. Sally was being "jumped into" the gang— all of the member girls got to hit her ten times each. I thought I had been transported to some deep, dark jungle to witness a tribal ceremony.

The girls all did a sort of jumping dance around the initiate, shouting in unison the number of the blow they were delivering to Sally. "One, two, three…" Round and round they danced. Sally was bigger than any of the other girls, but she did not fight them back. "…five, six, seven…" The counting was fast and furious. Only girls were allowed to

Photo 13 - Our Lady of Guadalupe Mural

initiate a girl, but I'll bet Sally was sore for a week after receiving about 50 girl-punches.

Now she was an official member of the new *Los* Homes Gang and everyone else would make her fights theirs in total disregard of Christian principles. Not that I had much hope of teaching these kids anything about Christian principles.

They had their own brand of morality:

"Thou shall not steal if anyone's watching."

"Lying is alright if you can do it loud enough to shout down the one accusing you and if there is no tangible evidence against you which the accuser may be smart enough to find."

"Thou shall not hesitate to do any sexual activity you can find a partner for."

"Any type of language is permissible in all circumstances if you feel like using it."

"Be sure to take anything anyone is willing to give, as long as you don't commit yourself to do anything in return."

I slumped onto the church steps and Hopie came up beside me. "How did you guys happen to start the gang?" I asked.

"Alfred, Li'l James, and I went to the store and James was getting all smart with the guy in the store. The guy twisted James' arm and threw him on the floor."

"Where were you guys all that time?"

"We were over looking at some stuff, but we heard the rumble and ran over. James was starting to cry so Alfred and I jumped in. We told that big guy to leave him alone. He said, 'No,' so we kicked his ass and he left James alone. We came out of the store and James slapped our hands saying, 'Alright, homeboys, that's the way the homes take care of themselves.' Ever since that day we started calling ourselves *Los* Homes."

As he finished the story, Hopie jumped up and ran over to talk to Fernando who had just come on the scene.

As I slipped into the rectory to end my day, I remembered having heard Filas use the term "homeboy" before. With it he referred to his fellow gang members, as though the community center where they have their headquarters is their home.

An hour later, Father Nolan was out making his nightly rounds of the buildings, checking to be sure the doors were locked. He found the doors of our meeting hall standing wide open, although I had carefully locked them. Upon further investigation he found that the California flag, a big silk one hanging from a pole on the stage, had been ripped off! Apparently some of the gang had managed to hide from me as I was locking the doors.

What an evening! It had started with the exhilaration of having a formal meeting with the kids and two trained social workers. Now I was wishing I could retreat into oblivion. Was I doing more harm than good? At least before this the kids were roaming the streets in two's and three's. Now I had turned loose on the world a united pack of trouble-seekers!

The next night Father Nolan asked me to help him in the parish hall by climbing the ladder to remove streamers while he held the ladder. As we worked, he lectured me on how useless it was for me to try to do anything with these gang kids. He reviewed how Brother Manuel, who had preceded me at this parish, had managed to avert a gang fight once, but that, in the long run, the only good his familiarity with the gangs did was enable him, when he saw a gang nickname on a wall to say with authority, "Smokie—Oh, yes, I know that guy; he's a VNE member."

Father Nolan continued, "Now take Mrs. Good as another example. She worked for 30 years as moderator of our fine teen club, but do even those good kids appreciate it? Nope. Once in a while a person asks if she's still around, but no one bothers to visit her or to send her a thank you note. So save your energy, Hilary; what good does it do?"

I felt like answering, "What good does it do for you to say Mass six days a week in a church empty except for a dozen old ladies, or to sit in the rectory taking care of only those people who come to you? Those are the good people, the ones who really don't need your help as much as most of the others." But I said nothing, since I believe in the infinite value of the Mass. Besides, Father Nolan was holding the ladder!

Photo 14 - Gang Artistry

13 WRESTLING WITH MY PROBLEMS

A few days later, I myself had the dubious privilege of being jumped into the *Los* Homes Gang! After school I was looking for some exercise and my ride to the tennis court did not materialize. I offered myself as center of a wrestling match for four of the toughest eighth graders in our parish school.

They did not succeed in getting me down to the concrete of the schoolyard, so I was still feeling pretty tough when six of my gang members came along. At least a couple of them were smaller than those eighth graders had been so I felt pretty confident. Once again I had not allowed for the sinewy toughness of my gang.

As their bodies clashed with mine, I could feel rock-solid muscle, none of the flabbiness of our school-boys. It did not take them many dives at me, two after each of my legs and one to occupy each of my arms, before they had managed the fall which many another wrestler had failed to work on me. I might well have smothered under the weight of those six wriggling bodies, but when I groaned "OK," they sprang up saying, "Now you're a member of *Los* Homes, Brother." They shook my hand and slapped me on the back. It was the most rewarding loss of my career!

That evening we had our first successful grunion hunt, but I was too busy driving to see the catch. Too many kids wanted to go. I had only one car so I made two trips. At twenty-five miles each way, that means I drove 150 miles before the evening was over.

While both carloads were at the beach, we caught only four fish, but while I was taking one load home, the other bunch struck it rich. They caught forty! That is one fish for every 3 ¾ miles I drove—before the 1979 OPEC energy crisis. They had one of the greatest evenings of their lives, splashing in the surf and groping in the sand among hundreds of wriggling, silvery treasures.

Good Friday was another memorable day. I asked a nice lady to take me and the gang to the nearest large group of tennis courts, the ones at East Los Angeles Junior College two miles away. There is usually a sort of hushed reserve on a Good Friday afternoon. Not so wherever the *Los* Homes Gang was. In fact we almost had a riot on two of the courts. The concentration of almost every other tennis player must have been shattered.

The trouble started when the boys lost interest in playing tennis. They started playing "basketball" using my fifty tennis balls and a trash can in the corner of one court. Balls were rolling all around and my crew was getting noisier and noisier. Then they had to start a war, everyone against everyone else, throwing balls at each other. Balls were flying onto other peoples' courts.

Finally I could stand it no longer. I grabbed the nearest kid, Fernando, around the waist and whirled him off of his feet with a sweeping motion so recklessly fierce that it landed him on my back with his back to my back. Thus, in a sort of inverted piggy-back style which made him look almost as helpless as a turtle on its back, I carried him to a nearby bench and plunked him down with "...and stay there!"

That was my mistake. Now I was playing his game, that of strong-willed violence. He was not about to stay on the bench. Now that I had started the tough stuff, I had to use enough of it.

He was trying to get away, so I grabbed him by his long hair, got a choke-hold on his neck, and wrestled him back to the bench. I was lucky the rest of the gang was not coming to his aid. They just stood around watching—like the people on the other ten courts.

As I sat there with my struggling victim, my mind had to figure some way of salvaging my relationship with the boys, and, incidentally, my own life. What would happen if I let Ferny go? Would he pull a knife on me, run around gathering tennis balls and flinging them as far as he could in every direction?

Or would he grab any rackets he could find and smash them to pieces on the concrete courts? I saw no possible way of returning to a tranquil tennis game and I did not relish the idea of having all the boys do a serious job of jumping me!

When Ferny was momentarily subdued, I got away from him like a man releasing a rattlesnake and insisted on shaking hands, while explaining to everyone how the spectacle had been disturbing the concentration of serious tennis players, and asked them to gather the tennis balls in preparation for departure.

There were a few tense moments, but no more confrontations. They did as I directed. As we moved toward the street to await our ride, a non-gang kid sidled up to me and asked, "Why do you mess with these gang kids at all, Brother Hilary?" All I could say was, "I guess I'm just a compulsive optimist."

The next day was Saturday. I took my day off without the kids and went all the way to Ensenada, Mexico for a change of scene. When I got back, I had to defend myself for not having taken them with me. In my absence they had stolen a paper from the front desk of the rectory and otherwise aggravated the secretaries and priests. The paper they had taken was a petition against the sale of spray paint to people under eighteen years of age.

Easter morning I had the job of standing in front of the church to solicit signatures for that petition. The gang members made things difficult by poking their noses in to see who was signing what petition and by trying to destroy the petitions since the petitions were directed at shutting down one of their favorite pastimes.

I think the gang was down on me. I did not see any members for a few days, but when I did I learned yet another facet of East LA gang life. Alfred came to a meeting hiding his hand in his jacket. It was rather obvious that something was wrong so I asked one of the other boys about it.

He said that Alfred, Li'l James, and Jesse had been jumped by members of the 3rd Street Gang. Alfred got cut by a knife so the three of them decided to accede to the demands of the jumpers, i.e., to give up their shoes. I found it hard to believe, but intensive questioning gave me the following picture.

The 3rd Street Gang, at least the group which jumped the boys, was made up of very poor guys, many of them having arrived in America only recently. Either they or their families were so desperate that they resorted to robbing rival gangs of their shoes.

This third meeting brought out an extraordinarily large number of gang members. About twenty-five of them were in the yard, sitting in dark corners drinking beer, sniffing paint, and, I feared, writing on the walls. If I could not stop them, this writing would mean extra work for our valiant caretaker in the morning.

Whenever there has been new writing on the walls, he goes out early in the morning and paints over it. The old paint has deteriorated in the smoggy atmosphere, so the fresh paint of varying ages makes the church walls look like a patch-work quilt as high as the kids can reach.

Only a few kids had come into the meeting with me and Gene Tanaka, but when we adjourned, we found the yard alarmingly full of dark shadows. I said to Gene, "You know, I sometimes wonder if we're not doing more harm than good by having these meetings. We bring all these thugs together and then there is more trouble than there would be if they were wandering the streets in two's or three's."

He had to agree that the thought had entered his mind. This time I was really worried since my past few brushes with the kids had not been ideal. And there were new faces in the darkest corners, as if some new evil influences were trying to infiltrate us and further the corruption. I sensed that if I asked them all to leave the yard, I would get either sullen disobedience or a riot.

I decided upon a daring move. Perhaps if Gene and I would walk up to the various groups and try to join the conversations, the groups would disperse. There must be a name for this phenomenon. It seems to me that anytime there is a potentially dangerous conversation going on in any group which is not yet well-organized, all an obvious outsider needs to do is walk up as if he wants to join in. Not only does the topic of conversation change, but usually the group starts to break up and move away. If I could use this device to disperse the gang quietly, it would be a major victory for a sociological pattern.

I was pretty sure it would work. I chose the largest group in the darkest corner and sent Gene to tackle the group gathered around obviously-stoned Filas. The scheme worked like a charm. Gene engaged Filas in conversation and soon the others drifted away. In my group I sat down beside the newcomer who also seemed to be the dispenser of beer and cigarettes. He introduced himself and started recounting "the good ol' days," i.e., when he was a member of one of the church teen clubs.

He recalled having started Filas and several others in the paint sniffing game years ago. "I quit, though," he said, "it messes you up. Poor Filas is a perfect example; he's an addict now. I like beer better." Soon everyone was gone except this guy Art and one of the older members of my gang, Jesse.

Art started asking questions about Brother Manuel who had been here about three years ago. That led to questions from Jesse about how the life of a Brother works, how it happens that Brother Manuel, born in East LA, should now be at our monastery in Oklahoma while, I, born in Oklahoma City, was working in East LA. I simply said that our Abbey had founded two parishes in the LA basin at the turn of the century and that Manuel had gone to Oklahoma to join the service of God, the church, and the people. The same reason had similarly led me to LA under the guidance of our Abbot.

As we talked, the explosive situation passed. Back in my room I thanked God.

When Gene Tanaka came to the church for our next weekly meeting with the kids, I saw Hopie. Gene had scheduled the meeting at the same time as I had to give a tennis lesson. I was just returning from that lesson as the gang meeting broke up. The kids were mad at me for seeming to prefer teaching tennis to coming to their meeting. Maddest of all were two girls Loca and Shorty.

Loca called me "Rockhead" and threw a firecracker near me while Gene and I were standing apart from the group to talk. We moved over beside them. Then Shorty held a firecracker while Loca lit it. I was standing just five feet from them. Shorty held the cracker in poised position, watching the fuse burn low enough. She tossed it toward my face. It went off midway between her and me and gave me one of the more memorable shocks of my life.

I was so furious that I lunged at her, put an armlock on her neck, and shook her violently. As I flung her away, I had the whole group mad at me. Gene tried to calm things down and started suggesting that the kids go on home.

Loca stood about twenty feet from me, bent her body toward me from the waist, threw back her head and shoulders and screamed, "Fucking Rockhead!" several times with all her might. I could not bear this, and started after her. That, along with Gene's renewed efforts to clear the yard, started the herd moving toward the schoolyard gate.

My ears were still ringing from the firecracker when Gene and I went into the rectory. We were soon joined by Hopie, Fernando, and Efren. "What happened, Brother?"

I could see trouble coming. Surely the boys would defend their fellow gang members. I did not know what approach to use. "Shorty and Loca threw a firecracker right at my face, so I grabbed Shorty and started wringing her neck."

"That's alright, Brother-man. We know how it is. Those girls always cause trouble." Their smiles showed how good they felt to be on the other side of trouble for a change. "Don't let it getcha down, Brother. How's about taking us cruising somewhere."

"Forget it, guys. I'm not in the mood right now."

"OK, Brother. We'll let you slide this time." They tramped noisily across the rectory lobby, jerked the door open, then slammed it behind them while ringing the doorbell three times and shouting, "We'll catch you later!"

Photo 15 - Gang Insignia

14 ATTEMPTING ANALYSIS

Several months of these exciting contacts with the gang, had made me very concerned about the kids' welfare. I was constantly watching for any facts which might help my understanding of their situation. Some interesting insights came from various things my Creative Writing pupils wrote.

My pupils in the school were the same age as the gang members, but came from families which were either richer or which considered the education we gave worth the monetary sacrifice.

Though none of my students were gang members, a few were what I call "Gang Sympathizers" and the lives of all were affected by gang life around them. Those few who were Gang Sympathizers used gang insignias in writing on desks or walls and even on the class papers they turned in.

Some adopted the proud, angular sort of printing upon certain occasions as though to slip into another personality, one which would cause others to look at them with awe and puzzlement as if to say, "Gosh, that's real cool writing. Are you really a gang member or do you have lots of tough friends who are?"

Here is what one of my pupils wrote concerning his relationship to the gangs. "Everybody thinks I'm from a gang, but I'm not. If I would join a gang, it'd be the LVJ, the Joker division of the Li'l Valley, because I know most of the guys from there. I don't like to write about LV because they might jump me, but I wouldn't get scared because I have friends from other gangs."

One very revealing characteristic of my pupils which made gang life more understandable is that many of them claimed to be totally bored with life. They live in the middle of a metropolitan population of about eight million people, surrounded by a great variety of characters, yet they are bored.

At times, I would assign topics for 50-word compositions, but the times when I left the topic open to their choice were those when I got the most blank stares. "Nothing ever happens to me, Brother. My life is just one duddy day after another."

Just one duddy day after another! In all my own life I can't recall long periods of having nothing to do. There were always interesting books to read or things to do in nature or outdoor games. But for these kids there is no nature, just miles and miles of concrete. Only a few children become interested in such rigid activities as gardening or pet-raising.

Their society seems to have no use for books. The students struck me as being very intelligent, but if their parents spoke mostly Spanish or "Spanglish," the students were not able to spell or to write English as well as they might. "I just go home and lie around listening to records," they told me.

"Why don't you read a good book?" I asked.

"Aw, they're not interesting."

If my students were so bored with life in the city, though leading such privileged existences compared to gang members, it seems clear that boredom and general inability to recognize any purpose in life must account for many attitudes displayed by gang kids.

Not all pupils were so bored with life, yet they could sense the problem in the lives of others. "I have a friend from a gang," one student wrote. "I don't like his gang because all his 'homeboys' [fellow gang members] knifed him. His nickname was Smokey. They knifed him all over his body, but he still lived. That was two years ago.

"Now he is dead because he hanged himself at his house because he said he didn't get anything out of life. He was dumb to hang himself. He had the guts to do it. If that were me I think I would have done it too. But I like my life. I was sad when he did it. I think more of my friends might do it too. It's for sure that I'm not going to hang myself because I'm enjoying my life with other persons."

Though urban boredom deserves some blame for youthful violence, it became more and more clear to me that the child's feeling of an absence of parental love and good example could often be blamed for the life of a gangland child.

Thus one of my school "Gang Sympathizers" wrote as follows. "On Christmas eve at midnight all the adults stay up throwing bottles in the street or eggs at cars that pass by, not all the cars, only those of some of our friends or uncles or aunts. At Christmas I got $2 and later my mother is going to buy me some pants and shirts.

"That's why I didn't cry like other people do. They are dumb if they start to cry because that's not the reason for Christmas. If you don't get anything, they still love you, the ones who don't give you anything." I suggest that this young man's ability to perceive love where some others of his age had seen none was at least part of what kept him out of the gangs.

Perception of love is like perception of anything else. Certain students seem unable to learn from certain teachers. Do we then condemn the teacher or the pupil? Some people would blame one, some the other. I would blame neither. I would simply try different combinations.

Put the student with other teachers until one is found whose love the pupil can relate to. In my own case, rather than blame parents for lack of love or gang kids for inability to respond to what love there was, I determined to do my best to show that I, at least, had great concern for them.

If boredom and lack of perception of that certain undefinable amount of adult love are the groundwork on which gang life is built, I suggest that prejudice and an overemphasis on sex are the framework of the superstructure. I had viewed this prejudice from the outside, so to speak, for most of my life before going to East LA, but once there I experienced it subjectively and in a two-fold manner.

My first memory of prejudice was of what I call the objective variety. When I was a child of about five, I remember that my mother hired a black lady to do some ironing for us. I wandered into the kitchen and, as soon as I spied the lady, I said, "You're a nigger aren't cha?" The lady quietly said, "No." But I insisted, "Yes, you are; you're a nigger."

My mother came in to find me making those proclamations. She promptly took me to another room for padding and a few words which I believe cured me for all time of prejudice and intolerance. As I grew older, I began to view prejudice as gross ignorance, as judging someone on the basis of exterior factors before taking the time to get to know that person as a human being.

I also experienced prejudice subjectively. I found that many people would shy away from me if I were wearing my robes on, for example, the campus of the University of Oklahoma where I did some graduate work. But if they got to know me first, then learned of my being a monk, they were always open and interested. Although I was close to being on the receiving end of prejudice, I could avoid it by varying my costume.

When I arrived in East LA, I found myself in a situation where I could not change my looks so readily. I was fair-skinned, though always tanned from tennis, and the hair which I had always thought of as being brown was now considered to be blonde by the Mexican-American people and I was branded, *huero*, gringo, paddy, Anglo, and even Okie if someone learned of my Oklahoma origin. For the first time, I experienced the helplessness of one who is the object of prejudice.

As I grew to love my pupils, I came upon a second facet of what I refer to as subjective knowledge of prejudice. I began to identify with my pupils more than I had ever done with any other minority group. Thus I felt something of their frustration when, for example, a TV program would use someone other than a full-blooded Mexican to portray a character who was obviously meant to be of Mexican descent.

It made me sick. The movie industry is using loads of new-name actors, making stars out of nowhere, yet there are certainly some Mexican-Americans trying to get into the movies, but who are ignored in favor of a gringo used to play a Mexican part.

Prejudice breeds not just prejudice, but a more intense and more refined type of prejudice. When a people is hated, it returns the hatred. But, when people can't shrug off the hatred and can do no harm to the ones who hate them, they begin to be more and more selective of the people they themselves will tolerate.

Soon they are rejecting people of their own heritage who have some difference from them or who have some resemblance to or affinity for the race which made them feel hatred in the first place. This is part of the reason why we find blacks and Chicanos warring among themselves.

On the preceding pages, I have described some aspects of prejudice in my story about our walk home from the community center. Here are some more, taken from the writings of my students. There are two major divisions.

1) *Feeling Anglo prejudice and reciprocating:*
"I live in East Los Angeles, that is, *El Este de Los Angeles*. It is the Gang Capital of the world. All the rest of the area of Los Angeles is full of paddies. Some are alright, but most of them are queers. Over here is where the Chicanos live. The people over here have to protect their rights because the other people try to push us around."

Again: "A paddie is a person who is a white and very mean. Their people are very prejudiced. They are always calling us Dirty Mexicans. The girls are so ugly that we are way prettier than they are. Their people think they're all good. The black and Chicano people are all the way, right, Brother?"

2) *Feeling Anglo prejudice and passing it on to others of Mexican heritage who are thought to be giving a bad name to the well-established Mexican-American:*
"I do not like the TJs because they are different from us. All they speak is Spanish. We might know how to speak Spanish, but most of us speak English. Every week they probably go to TJ.

"The reason some people make fun of TJs is because they're poor. A lot of people say a TJ is a person who looks like the *migra* (immigration authority) is after him. I think a TJ is more like this: they dress stupidly like green pants with blue blouse and high heels with short sox.

"A *cholo* is different from a TJ because the *cholo* wears dirty and torn clothing and walks with his arms going to the back. They get into gangs so they can go all around the city and write on the buildings. Sometimes they rob schools."

That was an amalgamation of comments by my students with reference to certain groups which the Mexican-American feels cause the Anglo to hate anyone of Mexican heritage without distinguishing TJs and *cholos* from longtime Mexican-Americans.

By the time a youth has grown up in an environment which makes so many prejudicial distinctions, he is habituated

Photo 16 - "Joe Blow" Illustrated

to such activities and so passes easily from condemning TJs, *cholos*, and paddys to denunciation of his own classmates or the people on the next block. This gives rise to much gang activity. One of my pupils wrote the following about his own classmates using the nickname of Joe Blow:

"I drew a picture of Joe Blow on an art paper and hung it up in the class. Joe got pissed off because in the drawing I drew his family swimming across the border. We call him *wetback* or m*ojado*.

"One of the guys made up a song about him and it goes like this. 'Hello, hello, hello, my name is TJ Joe. I am a *mojado*. I live in Mexico.' When someone was singing that song in class just before the bell rang, everyone started shouting together, 'Call the *migra*; call the *migra*.'

"We stamped our feet two times after each phrase and repeated it over and over. The room was rocking with sound and our teacher couldn't make us quiet until another teacher came in."

Of course much of this was done in jest and I was encouraged by such a show of creativity, but I still point to it as indicative of an undercurrent of prejudice even in these non-gang children and which exists to an even greater extent in the gang ranks.

As was shown in Chapter Eleven, a little bit of prejudicial name-calling leads rapidly to war and that is what gang life is. We hear frequently on the international news about deaths from guerrilla activity in various parts of the world. That is exactly what we have in East LA, but there is little recognition of it.

Sex has always been a cause for contention among men. But in civilized society men curb their passions by discipline. Where there is no restraint on sexual desire, especially in the vivacious years of youth, careless marriages occur and warfare breaks out because of disputes involving sexual partners.

Notice the intermingling of prejudice with sexual desire in the following quote from a 14-year-old boy.

"Today when I went to school, I looked at the girls first. So did everyone else. I saw a girl who is very cute and nice. She has class. I liked her so she never got out of my mind. But then, shit, I found out that she is going around with someone. I saw her coming with her guy, some little bitch who thinks he's a *cholo*. He probably is but he's still a little bitch and that isn't going to stop me from liking her."

Note that this time it is directed toward a classmate. Here's one more example of prejudice and unrestrained preoccupation with sexuality.

"I know a guy in the eighth grade who looks like a girl, acts like a girl, and, to top it off, is a boy. His name is Gerardo (El Queero) Quiviro, [name changed, but rhythm, rhyme, and poignancy have been preserved] but we really call him Fag.

"He's always sticking up for the girls, but he's the biggest kissy to the girls. He's all hard-up over Linda. He buys her whatever she wants. He's a disgrace to the guys in the eighth grade. His fucking stomach is as big as the ass of one of the teachers and that's big!"

Unbridled concern with sex, thinking of it as the most important and interesting part of life, leads to much going steady already in the 7th and 8th grades and to marriage or extra-marital child-bearing upon graduation from the 8th grade. Educations are halted and lives ruined. New babies are crowded into homes already on welfare.

I have seen the children of welfare parents growing up in an atmosphere which has no respect for education and no need for honest labor. I fear that their welfare living will breed them into a new generation of welfare recipients. I know that many such children consider their school days to be irrelevant. They simply don't listen to their teachers. With little education except in gang violence and crime, what kind of future can the world expect them to have?

One time I was at a teachers' meeting in another part of the town and I met Rudy Morales, a 27-year-old *veterano* from the *Primera* Flats gang, otherwise known as First Flats since Spanish and English are so interchangeable in East LA. The gang is so named because of its location along and around East First Street. This man had been trying to make some money by painting murals over the *placa*-ridden walls of East LA.

He told me how gang life was in the fifties and sixties.

"It's not like what it used to be when I used to lowride. Before it was just one big *varrio*. Nowadays there is a greater number of smaller groups." This leads to more skirmishes.

"We must go right into the problem [of gang warfare] and stop beating around the bush. You know, really look at a guy and say, 'Maybe that guy is like that, he lowrides or he's a goddamn hoodlum, a *cholo*, or whatever you wanna call him— it's only because we make him that way.' The people in school, the teachers, the people, they don't care about this guy because maybe he's dressed the wrong way; he's wearing the wrong type of shoes. And this is what we have to overcome.

"We have to give him something to identify with other than just gang activity. This graffiti art [mural painting] is alright, but we have to make the young Mexican-American realize that there's not only just painting to be done, but a little bit of money to be made, that there's something else to look forward to. He's got a lot of other hidden talents. We don't need gang activity."

I had to break in with a theory I had heard used often, "What about the Latin's supposed need for violence to express his masculinity, that attitude known as *machismo*?"

"Aw, we don't *need* it, man. Gang fighting is alright when you're young, but when you start getting older, it gets too serious. The last fight I went to, I was 26 years old and my best friend got stabbed in the heart and died right there on the floor in front of my eyes. I've lost a lot of my friends like that. We don't need it; we don't need gang activity. What we need is a lot of athletic activity and some decent jobs."

Photo 17 - Brother Hilary Teaching Tennis

15 TENNIS ANYONE?

When summer came, Hopie and company had more time for tennis and seemed to enjoy pounding the ball around the schoolyard as long as I was doing it with them. But the moment I turned my back they lost interest. Even when I played with them, I could not pin them down enough to teach them many of the serious principals of tennis.

The nearest tennis courts were ten blocks away so I started outlining a tennis court on the pavement of the schoolyard. I used the watered-down paint residue left from the cleaning of paintbrushes. (My summer assignment at the parish was the painting of classrooms.)

To my surprise, I found that having a court marked off, even without a net, was a great help. It gave the kids some visible guidelines and a challenge to do something other than see how far they could smash the ball.

Of course my boys were still not committing themselves; in fact not a one of them had ever stuck to it long enough to play a full set. Soon we had three courts marked off. But all the courts in the world would not help if I could not get Hopie interested.

One day an eighth grade Japanese boy walked into the schoolyard with a gleaming metal racket. All he knew was that he wanted to learn to play tennis and that it took a ball, a racket, and a wall. The yard had plenty of walls.

I promptly cornered him and showed him the right way to do a few things. That was all it took. His disciplined personality led him to practice by the hour—alone against a wall. His example drew others into the sport. Soon every wall in sight felt the thud of tennis balls.

Hopie and the gang showed a sort of awe. How could that Japanese boy be so methodical, so serious about that little ball? They tried making fun of him, but he kept his cool, smiled quietly, spoke politely, and went on pounding the wall.

Soon Hopie and Fernando or Li'l James and Alfred would come to me asking to borrow a racket even though I was busy doing something else. Yet their attention spans were short. If a girl walked by or some other gang member rode through the yard on his bike, the rackets clattered to the ground and off they went.

For the few minutes of play their conversation would go something like this.

Hopie: "Let's play some tennis." He hits the ball to Fernando on the netless tennis court.

Fernando hits one back in Hopie's direction but so wide that Hopie misses it. Fernando says, "You fucking coulda reached it."

Hopie remains silent and shows his utter disdain for such pedestrian activity as chasing balls by letting the ball go 25 yards, all the way to the other end of the schoolyard. He maintains an aloof silence, typical of his leadership technique.

He hits the second and last ball to Fernando. Back to him it comes. A little rally is in progress. Hopie returns to Fernando. But then Fernando's return sails over Hopie's head to join the other ball at the far end of the yard. "The fucking thing goes too far," is Fernando's excuse.

"I'm goin' to the store," says Hopie and he casts his racket on the schoolyard bench!

Fortunately the boys' interest in the game gradually increased and I will never forget the day and the discipline involved when Hopie played his first set of tennis there in the yard. Other members of the gang would walk through the yard saying, "Come on Hopie; let's go to the store," but his desire to play a private game with me made him ignore them. He showed signs of being sorely tempted to leave, but he stuck with the game.

Even the scoring and the mental concentration required to learn where and when to move on the court, demanded of him more discipline than he seemed ever to have been accustomed to. My impression was that he was very intelligent, but just had no experience whatsoever in forcing himself to do something unfamiliar or contrary to whatever whim might pop into his head.

As we finished that set, big Alfred showed up and after a bit of consultation like, "I'll play you, Hopie," and, "Aw, you fat slob; you couldn't beat nobody," they demanded that I referee their tennis duel. I had many other players to be concerned with, but if I tried to step away for an instant I got, "Come back, Brother; he's cheating me."

Alfred managed to eke out the win in a tie-breaker and Hopie was very disconsolate. But I encouraged him by telling him I had always considered him to be the better player and that I had been afraid the other guys would be too sure of losing to him to ever play him again.

I heard that the National Junior Tennis league might be of help to a group like mine. And it was. The league readily adopted my schoolyard team and gave us dozens of rackets and balls. They even gave us shirts saying, "NJTL—Los Angeles."

By the next day the word had spread that I had free shirts for all tennis players. Suddenly the gang kids were interested:

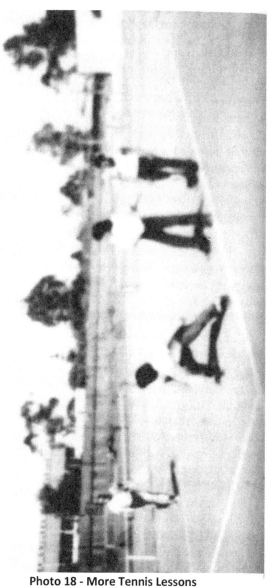

Photo 18 - More Tennis Lessons

six from *Los* Homes, two from the Li'l Valley, and one from *Primera* Flats.

I scheduled a tournament for the following Saturday and said that anyone who participated would get a shirt if he knew by then how to keep score and where to stand on the court.

I let them all use the new rackets. Since my previous experiences had shown a tendency toward kleptomania in the gang kids, I feared the racket supply might dwindle rapidly. When that did not happen, I recorded another point toward the civilization of my charges!

16 GUSSY MORAN

The NJTL leaders had told me that famed Gertrude "Gussy" Agusta Moran, who had wowed Wimbledon back in the '50s, had a group of ladies out in Santa Monica who would come and help me instruct my kids in tennis. I called Gussy (often misspelled as "Gussie") early the next morning to see if her ladies would come to coach on the sidelines while my Saturday tournament was going on.

She asked first what kind of facilities I had and when I told her about our makeshift resources, she was willing to try to find us some net posts and nets. She gave me hopes which started me on a really "up" day, and while I spent the day painting class-rooms, the yard outside was hopping with such an interest in my tennis program that kids were constantly coming to ask me for a tennis racket.

Even the paint sniffers from Li'l Valley came to play a bit and when they heard me singing the "Our Father" through the open window of the classroom, to my utter amazement, they joined in for a few verses.

Later in the day I marveled as a rain of tennis balls came off the roof of the school where the boys had thrown them

Photo 19 - Brother Hilary and Gussy Moran

weeks before. Some kids new to the program tried to make off with the booty but I heard little Peewee's high-pitched voice shouting, "Hey, don't take those; those balls belong to Brother Hilary." Then with the authority typical of a gang member over non-members, he made the rounds of the kids who had retrieved the balls, gathered a full armload of the beat-up old things, and marched over to give them to me!

The next day Gussy Moran called me to say that she had found two discarded tennis nets and that all I had to do was arrange to pick them up.

Later, she came in the flesh with her beautiful protégé, Nancy Zimbalist, daughter of actor Efren Zimbalist, Jr. I scarcely had time to meet them; I was so busy that day arranging matches for the kids. Since we had about thirty participants, but courts for only six players at a time, there were always twenty-four kids for the ladies to take into a corner and teach some theory to.

Gussy found a cul-de-sac and had some kids firing serves while Nancy spread out another group and demonstrated basic strokes. Thus we busied the kids until about noon when the ladies decided to quit. Gussy wiped clean a portion of a smog-covered bench and sat down. She studied the scene for a while, then asked what she could do to help the program.

Obviously the nets were in need of better support. So she promised to work on obtaining some kind of portable net post. She also volunteered to get us scads of balls since I had lost about thirty that day. She even promised to help teach again in two weeks. I gratefully accepted all such offers.

When the ladies were gone, I passed out the shirts saying, "National Junior Tennis League—Los Angeles." I noticed happily that Hopie and the other *Los* Homes members had done very well in the day's competition; they had won about three-fourths of their matches.

17 BAREFOOT IN THE PARK

The rectory cook is not on duty Sunday evenings so everyone must fend for himself. On this particular occasion I had arranged to have a picnic with a brother-sister couple I knew: Donna and Joe.

I picked them up and headed for Echo Park since Donna loved ducks and there are dozens of them on a beautiful lake in that park. We spread some huge towels in the sun on a hill over the water and proceeded with our picnic. We had almost finished eating when a group of five late-teens moved in nearby. They spread out a blanket but did not stay with it long.

Soon one of the two husky young men came over to offer us a pair of sparkling red and black platform shoes for $5. I gracefully refused saying, "They're well worth that much, but I haven't enough money." I had never seen such a pair of shoes before. Either it was the latest style or it was a style worn only by people I had no contact with.

I thought of how my school pupils had described the gaudy styles worn by TJs. Perhaps those were the type of shoes my pupils called Imperials, a pointy-toed style which

Photo 20 - *Cholo* and *Cholas* with Mural

they jokingly called "*cucaracha* killers" in a suggestion that TJs are so dirty as to have lots of cockroaches in their houses.

I was in the process of telling my friends how the 3rd Street gang had jumped my boys to get their shoes when we received another visit: a member of the same party, a girl in Levis and a silk print halter top sauntered up to us and said, "Hey, man, you got somethin' to drink?"

"No," was my reply, but she quickly pointed to our open grocery sack saying, "Yes you do, right in here." She was speaking loudly and in such a perturbed manner that her friends were starting to move toward us, especially when she said, "Hey, guys, look what they've got here."

"Let's get out of here," my instinct forced me to tell my friends.

But Donna's love for ducks and ignorance of gangs made her say, "Oh, let's stay a little longer."

We sat there while the gang converged upon us.

I had been clutching my borrowed camera and tape recorder from the moment of first contact. It dawned on me that I could not bear to face my fellow monks from whom I had borrowed them, if I let them be stolen.

I could wait no longer. I jumped up and started gathering as much as I could carry. Joe was calmly getting to his feet. Donna was still sitting. We had waited too long. The biggest girl had stepped into the middle of my towel and folded her arms as though to hold it like a fort until her comrades should arrive to handle us.

I was not about to wait that long. I had to get out of there with the equipment. Rather than push the girl off the towel, since that would certainly be construed as the start of a fight, I jerked the towel from under her. I thought she might go flying in the air. She certainly did.

I am noted for my speed, but had neglected to secure my gear for proper running. With camera, tape recorder, and towel dangling, along with one of our bags of groceries, I began to feel hopeless when one of the big *cholos* appeared to be rapidly heading to cut me off. I had heard of people being jumped in parks before. Now it was my turn!

I wanted to get to our car, but then I remembered that we had locked it and I did not have the key. I ran across the street oblivious of traffic. The big *cholo* was upon me as I reached the first car. Its window was open. I dumped everything into the open window and did not even have time to turn before the pummeling began.

He was flailing at my head with blows from every direction. I was down in an instant as the other one joined in from the rear. If I had thought the ground would be safer, I was dead wrong. These guys were not kidding.

They had not heard of the saying, "Don't kick a man when he's down," for the next blows were kicks—rained on my head as if I were the floor under a flamenco dancer. I finally opened my mouth to say, "That's enough." They failed to agree. I began to wonder if they were ever going to stop. They might stomp me to death. They were not even giving me a chance to put up my defenses.

I finally decided it was about time to start yelling for help. "Heeeelp!" I screamed and my voice sounded weak and far away. Really, it did. I tried it again; it came louder. "Heeelllppp." I was aware of people watching, but they were not doing anything. Even cars were stopping for the show—just like at a drive-in theater! They were stacking up in all four lanes of Echo Park Avenue!

Suddenly it was all over. They became afraid of the crowd. "Let's get out of here!" they shouted.

As my assailants were leaving, one guy reached into the car for our bag of groceries, the easiest thing to see, and started to run down the sidewalk. Still screaming for help, I gave pursuit. My only hope for stopping him was a flying tackle and I had sworn off those after eighth grade. But I wanted this big guy badly. My camera might even be in that sack. So I flew. The picnic goods spewed everywhere as we both landed hard on the cement. I felt stunned.

I came to, to find the *cholos* gone. Joe and Donna were gathering up the groceries for a hasty departure. "Where were you two?" I asked.

"I had to take care of Donna," said Joe. As we came to the car with the open window, I was relieved to see my borrowed equipment was still where I had tossed it.

I slumped dazedly into the back seat of Donna's car thinking, "So that's what it's like to be jumped by a gang. I'm lucky they didn't have knives!"

When we got to the traffic light at the end of the block, we found ourselves stopped right beside a police car. I leaned out of the window and said, "Hey, man, where were you when I was getting the hell beat out of me just now?"

"Where'd it happen?" he asked.

"Right back there at the park."

"Are the assailants still there?"

"I don't know, but we can look."

"Would you recognize them?"

"Sure."

He told us to follow him and as we drove around the block I wondered how the cops could have possibly been at that light without having seen my beating. Maybe we were a little slower getting into the car than I had realized. The police stopped just around the corner from the park and told me to get into the car with them. Donna and Joe were begging me not to get involved with the law.

The officers cruised slowly along Echo Park Avenue while I scanned the park with little hope. Then, to my great surprise, I spotted the five. They were walking casually beside the water not 100 yards from the scene of our original contact.

"There they are!"

"You sure?"

"Sure I'm sure."

The policeman drove right up over the curb and parked with the rear wheels still in the street. He took a few steps toward the youth and shouted, "Hey, you guys, come here." I stayed low in the car lest they should spot me, know they were in trouble, and all run in different directions.

As it was, they thought they were safe so they sauntered up to the officer saying, "Yeah, man, what'cha need?"

I could not hear what the officer said but their reply was audible enough. It was the kind of lying protest I had become familiar with in the lives of my own "gangsters." "Hey, man, we just barely got here, man." But the officer promptly cuffed the two boys together and told the girls to sit down on the hill. The silk-topped girl noisily refused until a little force was used.

I stayed in the car while the officer passed between me and the kids to check my story against theirs and vice-versa. Two or three other cars arrived so that the whole scene posed a good show for the people hanging off their balconies across the street in the two-and-three-story apartments.

Finally the girls too were cuffed and all five were squeezed painfully into the back seat of one car while I was kept in my original seat.

Next stop was the LAPD's Rampart Division. I could not believe this was actually happening to *me*. But there I was driving into the parking lot of police cars and entering the back door of perhaps the most famous police station in the world.

Inside there was a large room with about 25 gray-topped desks, mostly vacant that Sunday evening. My assailants were making noisy disavowals to the officers: "Hey, man, we didn't do nuttin. What's this all about? What are we supposed to a done?" The funniest thing (to me) was when they finally got a good look at me and said, "Who's this guy? Did something happen to him?"

I was directed to take a seat at one of the desks and to write and sign a statement to the effect that I was hereby performing the arrest and that the officers were merely providing transportation.

We left the three girls in that room as the two boys and I were moved toward the front of the building. They were put into some locked rooms with heavy wire windows and I was dismissed to call my friends for a ride home.

While I was waiting for my ride, I decided that the best way to part company with my assailants was not the way enemies part. I asked the officer at the desk if I could speak to the guys whom I could see through the office door. "No consulting with prisoners kept here," he said. "When they're transferred to the jail, you may speak with them."

Since these young men were of Mexican descent, I thought they might be Catholic so I wrote them a note saying, "Hi, guys, I'm a Brother of the Catholic Church. I'm sorry for the inconvenience I've caused you and I forgive you for any harm done to me. Sincerely, Your Brother."

Fearing they might not be as conciliatory as I, I deliberately did not give my name or any indication of where I was from. I took the note to the man at the desk and asked him to give it to the boys. "No notes," he said.

I was really mad. Here I was trying to soften the hearts of some criminals, rather than let this experience harden them, and I was given no chance. I argued with the officer. No luck.

Since I could see the young men through the doors, I waved the note and showed them the peace sign. One motioned to the back door to suggest I enter there. I went to the back thinking I might at least find one of the officers I had dealt with. I thought I might slip in and make it far enough in to give the note to the *cholos*, but I was deterred by the thought that I would probably then be caught and locked up with them.

Near the back door, on top of one of the police cars, was a paper sack I recognized. It contained the shoes which had started everything. What poetic justice, I thought, that these shoes should now fall into my hands as a keepsake. I grabbed them up and ran around the building, stashing them in the bushes until my ride could arrive.

Back out front I sat on the bench inside the door. A few moments later, an officer escorted the girls out the front door. Because I had a message to deliver, I quelled my anger at the thought that they were going to be free from this place even before I was!

I gave the note to them just as they stepped out the door. An officer and a door were between me and them. I sat anxiously waiting for them to finish reading it. Would they scoff at it, become angry again, or accept my offer? Then one of them poked her head in through the door and said, "Hey, man, we're sorry. We're Catholic too. We didn't mean any harm. You just shoulda given us something to drink." I stepped outside and proceeded to have a long chat. Finally we all waved at the prisoners and then the girls started walking for home.

18 ONE SCRAPE TO ANOTHER

All I had to show for my experience was a big, deep scrape on the side of my wrist where I had slid on the concrete while tackling one of the thugs, but my chest bones ached so much that I could barely take a deep breath.

That scrape needed a bandaging. My wound was oozing worse than at first and I knew the rectory had no provision for dressing such a wound. I remembered a lady named Grace who keeps her house open all night to give comfort to the members of the Li'l Valley gang after their head-quarters, The *Casa Esperanza*, closes.

Filas had introduced me to her when he had become convinced that I would really like to do something to help the gangs. On the night when I had first met her, Grace had said, "I just sit here all night and bandage their wounds and try to convince them not to do any more driving when they come in all stoned. This is the gang's night headquarters. I open up when the community center (one of many around East LA) closes."

"Why are you so interested?" I had asked.

"Because two of my sons and one of my daughters are in the gang."

This reminded me of Hopie's own father who told me that he has six sons, all in different gangs. "Why do you let them be in it?"

"How can I stop them? They could be members without my permission. Besides, if they go to school and are recognized as being from this territory, it's assumed they belong to this gang so they get beat up unless they have the protection which fellow gang members can give them."

"Why don't you just move away?"

"Because I like it here. This is where I grew up and I'm not letting anyone tell me where to live. Anyway, it costs too much to move."

As I sat there that night conversing with Grace, she had introduced me to her daughter and some friends. They were all typical heavily made-up *cholas*, sitting around the house on a Saturday evening while waiting for the *cholos* to come back from a bachelor party.

One of them had asked me how I happened to get involved with gangs so I mentioned the *Los* Homes Gang. At that, Grace's daughter seemed to awaken from a semi-torpid state of boredom. "The *Los* Homes Gang, eh? You mean the one with Hopie and Efren?"

"Yes."

"Hey, man, that's my gang. My nick-name is Sad-Girl."

"You mean you're not in Li'l Valley?"

"Nope. I hang around with a different bunch—you know, Chica and Rosie and Negra."

I had recognized the names, but even after all this time with the Homes Gang, I could not put the nicknames with all the real people I knew. In fact here was a member I had never even heard of, Sad-Girl. "Welcome to the gang," I had said, "I'm a member too. I got jumped in several months ago. Of course, I try to steer the gang into more socially friendly behavior than your ordinary gang. I'm teaching them tennis and finding jobs."

"Can you find me a job?" she had asked.

"I'm afraid it's too late for this summer, but I can give you some leads for next."

That conversation was the background I had had, along with general knowledge of the Li'l Valley Gang's activities, before I arrived at Grace's house the evening after my "accident." I had met several members of the gang and was particularly well acquainted with Filas.

This evening I parked in front of the house and walked right into the front room, passing between several *cholos* who were standing around on the front lawn. The front door was open and as I stepped into the house, I asked, "Where's Gracie? I've got a wound for her to bandage."

"She's gone to the hospital," murmured a young man who was pacing back and forth on the living room floor with his head down.

"So, who would like to bandage my wounds?" I asked light-heartedly.

"I don't think anyone's in the mood to do that right now," said the other. "Three of the girls just got shot."

"Where'd it happen?"

"Right here. They were standing out front when some guys drove by and shot at them. They've got this place marked. I knew it'd happen, but why the girls?"

"Was Sad-Girl one of them?" I asked.

"You know her? Yeah, she was one."

A really big fellow came out from one of the back rooms. "I'll kill those bastards," he roared at the top of his lionish voice. He raised both of his clenched fists and nearly touched the ceiling even though his arms were bent with tension. "How low can they be, shooting girls?" With that he bashed his fist against the frail door he had come through.

The pacing fellow pointed to the spot hit by the fist-smasher. "You can see the shotgun pellet marks on the walls. They came in through the window."

It began to dawn on me that with open window, open door, and gun-toting people driving around shooting at the house, this was not exactly the safest place to get my wound dressed! But I wanted to show my concern.

I walked over to examine the place where the pellets had hit. It was on the door in the back wall of the room. Almost a perfect circle about 1 ½ feet in diameter had been formed by pellets which hit about 1/3 of an inch apart from each other.

I walked back over to the young man. "What gang did it?"

"We don't know if it was *El Hoyo Mara*, Geraghty *Lomas*, King Kobras, or *Varrio Nuevo*; those are the gangs we don't get along with."

I stepped outside where I now realized the guys in front were also pacing, trying to think of a next move. I was in the middle of a war!

Just then some tires squealed violently out front. Everyone was moving fast and I knew where I was going. I hugged the little piece of wall between window and door. It was only about four feet wide.

Most of the gang members had leapt out of the light streaming from the house. It made them perfect targets. One of the boys in the room with me dove onto the couch and jerked the cord to put out the light. A pang of mortal dread, such as I had never experienced before, shot through my heart.

Then someone shouted: "It's just Filas." He had rushed back from the hospital to lead any attack and to tell us that none of the girls were considered to be in a dangerous state.

"Thank God for that," came from several corners.

I hope I did not look like I was crouching too low, like one crawling through a foxhole, but that's the way I felt as I ducked into my car and forced myself to drive calmly away.

I still had no bandage on my arm and I could not go to bed until I did have. I decided to visit the home of Mrs. Sanchez. She was entertained by my gang stories while she did her work of mercy on my arm. "Good heavens," she purred, "it just gets worse and worse every day. It's just not safe for ordinary people to do anything anymore. My friend Sylvia is taking her child Felipe out of the public school next year. You know Felipe don't you, Brother?"

"Yes. He's one of my more faithful CCD pupils."

"Well, they say they can't afford the Catholic school, but they'll have to if they want Felipe to be safe."

19 THE CALL OF GOD

I had now got to the stage where my boys were playing well-disciplined tennis and, by their example, were keeping the tennis program active. When they came back in the evening, after their working hours and mine, they would say: "Come on, Brother. Play us a game now; you have time."

The spur for their desire was that we were preparing for the warming-up tournament of the National Junior Tennis League. It was late July and the real tournament to select players for the national tournament would not be until mid-August, but soon we would get to test ourselves against the rest of LA's players.

The day before the tournament came, the gang kids were challenging each other excitedly to a tennis game on one of the three schoolyard courts.

A lady from the *Casa Maravilla* community center came to check up on my workers. "They're part of my Neighborhood Youth Corps group," she said, "and I'm supposed to see what kind of work they're doing."

We surveyed the scene and I interpreted it for her. "As you can see, they're helping me run a recreational program.

We have rackets donated by the National Junior Tennis League and the kids help me put up the nets and they show other kids about the game of tennis which was considered 'sissy' around here until guys like Hopie and Fernando started playing." The lady seemed impressed so I went on. "And when they get tired of tennis I move them indoors to help me paint the school classrooms."

"Very good," she said, "I'll have someone bring over their pay-checks this afternoon."

"Thank you," I said, "and good luck with your other groups."

No sooner had she left than I was called into the house for a phone call. I ran in breathlessly and the secretary whispered, "Long distance."

I stepped into an office and shut the door. "Hello."

"Brother Hilary, this is Father Abbot."

"Well, well, fancy hearing from you."

"Brother, I want you to pack your things and come back home to the monastery."

I gasped, then stammered, "What's wrong? Don't you think I'm doing a good job here?"

"We'll talk about that when you get here. Call us from the airport and we'll pick you up."

"Father Abbot," I stammered, choking over the realization of all the programs I would be leaving on such short notice, "does it matter that the High School whose tennis team I've been coaching has offered me a job teaching math in the fall?"

"Well, I want you out of there right now so pack everything and we'll consider the fall when it gets here."

I had some errands to do in the afternoon and by evening I had figured out how I would tell the kids. I would just blurt out the news and then answer their *why*'s with simple facts. I did.

"You've been disturbing everyone in the rectory," I said, "and the secretaries are so upset that they're threatening to quit if something isn't done. So they figure that if they move me away, you guys will no longer come around."

"But what about the tournament?"

"I'll take you to that tomorrow and if you do well I'll ask Gussy Moran to take care of you on the next day and again on August 15th."

"What about our jobs?" That came from Hopie, from his pocketbook.

"Well, I know a guy at East LA College who teaches tennis all afternoon. Maybe I can arrange with him and the community center people to let you work with him as your director."

"Do you have to go, Brother?"

"Yes, my boss said to."

"But you could quit that job."

"Being in the monastery is not like an ordinary job; I'm not working for the Abbot, I'm working for God and whatever the Abbot says is the best thing for me to do."

The kids stood around me with mystified looks as I sat there on the schoolyard bench. Their rackets drooped silently to the ground.

"Let's write a letter of protest to the Abbot," someone suggested.

"Yeah," all agreed.

"Don't bother," I objected. "I'll already be in Oklahoma before your letter can get there." I rose. "Gotta go pack," I said. "You guys practice some more tennis for a while and I'll see you in the morning."

Saturday finally dawned, the big day for me to see under competition what I had accomplished with these kids. I felt optimistic about our chances in the tournament, but a peculiar aching somewhere between my heart and my stomach reminded me that this was to be my last full day with them.

It was a splendid day. The kids woke early and started swamping the schoolyard by eight o'clock. Not just my gang kids would be in this tournament, but anyone I had been teaching—at parks, at high school, and our own junior high. Even parents and older high school players were on hand to help transport us to USC.

When we finally arrived at the University, the scene was one of pandemonium. It was the least organized tournament I had ever seen! About 300 kids were crawling all over the block-long tennis facility.

The ten and twelve year olds were first to play, so Hopie and the *Los* Homes Gang had to wait all morning. I was afraid they would go wild in the crowd, but instead they sort of watched it like a show, amazedly. For once they were seeing a bigger riot than they usually produced.

At last we got our chance to play. Fernando was first on the court. He was appalled at the lack of discipline of his opponent. "Brother, he's cheating me. He's standing inside the court to serve and he calls them out when they're in."

"What's the score?" I asked

"I don't know. He thinks he's winning me, but he doesn't know how to keep score."

I had to stay at that court to help keep the rules. Under legal conditions, Fernando won easily.

When that match was over, I found silent Efren. "Did you win?" I asked. Even victory didn't open his mouth, but his vigorous nod and sparkling eyes conveyed the meaning.

Not everyone had been so lucky. Alfred and Li'l James lost in doubles. "They cheated us, Brother."

I couldn't help but notice the irony of my kids being so suddenly concerned with fair play. "How so?" I said, wondering if they had really learned the rules properly themselves.

"They let the same guy serve all the time and he kept stepping on the line," Alfred said. I was impressed.

We all settled down to watch Hopie's match. He was just as great as I had expected. Full of the competitive spirit, he raced all over the court in his bid for his first tournament win. The most undisciplined kid I had ever known was now pure business. Not a smile on his face, not even a glance at his audience, with his teeth set in grim determination, he silently and methodically demolished his opponent.

My little friend Felipe had entered the tournament and was now sitting beside me, cheering for the gang kids he had once thought so hopeless. "We're really doing good, Brother, and the *cholos* do even better than the other kids."

"Yeah, I always knew they could do it with a little guidance," I mused, "but I don't know what will happen to them when I'm gone."

Fernando broke in, "That dude's foot-faulting, Brother."

"That's OK," I said. "Hopie's beating him anyway so it's not worth fighting about."

When the match was over, Hopie came off the court like a real champion, not gloating, just glowing all over with the inner exhilaration of one who has "done himself proud."

The kids slapped his hand shouting, "Give me five, man." Then we all headed for the scoring table to check our team standings.

The charts showed that we had played about 35 matches and had won about 25 of them. It was impossible to tell for sure in the jumble at the scorer's desk, but it seemed that we had tied for second place among the approximately twenty teams participating.

"We gotta come back tomorrow, Brother," said Felipe. "The winners keep on playing each other."

"I know," I said, "but you'll have to come with somebody else because I've got to pack."

"How will Hopie and Fernando get here?"

"Well, if you can get your mother to bring you they can ride with you."

"OK, Brother, but you arrange things."

On the way home I praised the boys for their success and tried to organize their future development. "You guys come to the schoolyard tomorrow at 9 and Felipe's mother will give you a ride to USC."

The boys were strangely silent so I seized the opportunity and said, "Let's say a prayer."

"Oh God, thanks loads for the help today. We knew we could do it with Your help. Please continue to help us tomorrow and in the following weeks as we try to do everything, even tennis, for the advancement of Your kingdom on earth. We ask these things through Christ our Lord."

A few disheartened *amen*'s were audible.

"Are you sure you can't take us tomorrow?" Fernando asked.

"Absolutely," I said. "Today was my day off, tomorrow I pack, Monday I leave. Do your best tomorrow, but don't worry if we're not the top team this time because the real tournament is August 15th. Gussy Moran has promised to come on the next two Saturdays to prepare you, and if you win that tournament you'll get a free ride to the Nationals in Cincinnati and Washington, D.C."

Too bad all days can't go so well. The next morning was a different story. I glanced up from my busy packing while mothers came to take the kids to the tournament. Hopie and the *Los* Homes Gang did not show up at all, but I couldn't take time to try to roust them out.

"I guess they just won't do anything without you, Brother," Felipe said.

"They'll have to learn to," I replied. "Their protest is hurting no one but themselves."

On the following day it was time for me to catch a plane. Hopie came early to the rectory door. "Where shall we work today, Brother?"

"Come on in and I'll phone some people to see what we can get set up." I managed to arrange for them to help with the tennis program at East LA College.

"But that's nearly two miles from here," Hopie objected.

"I can't help it; you'll just have to take the initiative and ride the bus there. If you can't do that, it's just too bad, because I can't be here any longer. Now let me take your pictures before I go."

It was then that I learned about *cholo* picture taking. If they have the picture taken while they're standing, they use a toes-outward stance. The way they stand is very haughty. Often, however, they prefer to be photographed in a defiant sort of crouch.

While the camera clicked from different angles, Li'l James wrote me a sort of going-away card by putting many of the gang nicknames on a paper. "This is my best gang writing, Brother," he said.

Hopie got the idea and put his name on a separate page. I noticed that he spelled his name "Hopey" I asked why.

"'Cause somebody told me that girls spell their names with 'ie'."

"Well," I said, "You certainly are man enough to not let that worry you."

He smiled and we shook hands. "I've gotta go, guys, so don't ring the bell here anymore. God bless you all."

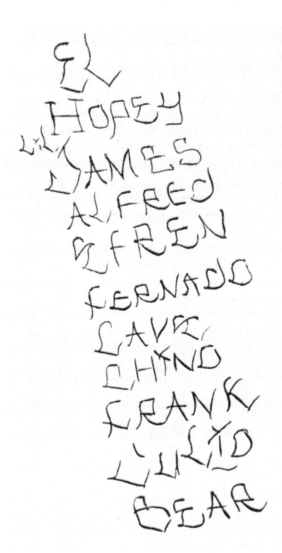

Photo 21 - Farewell Signatures

"You're trying to separate us, huh; well you can't do it, Brother." Anyway, what a waste of man-power the Big Brother program is, when each volunteer could be directing 10 to 20 kids in socially rewarding behavior.

Personally I can't think of any value in life I'd rather pass on to a young person than belief in, and service of, the Lord and of our fellow men. Therein lies the only key to a happy life. But my convictions cannot and must not be forced upon others, especially not upon people who have a culture extremely different from mine. Yet this key to a happy life is universal and we can hope to foster belief in this value by simple acts of love.

We so often get caught up in minutiae and lose sight of the big picture. Hopie and his friends will never be able to appreciate the Mass or any other religious service until they can relate religion to Jesus dying for love of them. But they will never understand the death of Jesus 2,000 years ago unless they find Him in someone ready to die for them— NOW.

While the Lord wanted me to remain in LA I tried my best to be like Jesus among them. This book is my way of continuing my presence there. It has cost me dear, but it will be worth the trouble if I find a few courageous people to whom I can pass the baton.

Where are you, Hopie and thousands like you?

You are walking the dark streets tonight, living in the shadow of danger and of death. At any moment a bullet may cut off your young life. I have done what I could and I have been following you since with my love and my prayers.

But, who is ready to take my place?

If you would like to assist in this vital work, please contact any of many church youth groups in the LA area.

AFTERWORD

So many years have passed that some events and dates are shaky. This is an update as recalled in November 2011.

You may recall that Felipe was the only one of the boys to participate in the NJTL tournament. I learned later that Felipe won at least one match there.

Felipe went on to play under his real name Philip Gutierrez at Cantwell High School in Montebello, CA. Philip attended Notre Dame University where he continued to play tennis mostly for recreation and exercise. He returned to Los Angeles to get his law degree at UCLA in 1984 and then practiced law for several years.

In 1997, California Governor Pete Wilson appointed Philip Gutierrez to be a Superior Court judge. Philip has called me through the years to stay in touch. He told me that in perhaps 1999, a young man named Hopie Lopez, Jr. appeared on his docket. He recognized the name and after consultation, he strongly suspected it was Hopie's son.

So ethics required that he recuse himself. He had to let another judge take the case. The fear in such cases is that the judge, having had experience with the family, might be prejudiced either for or against the young man.

In January 2007 Philip called to tell me he had been nominated by President Bush to be a United States District Court Judge for the Central District of California in Los Angeles. He was confirmed by all Democratic and Republican Senators and has been enjoying that job ever since.

Sadly, most of the *cholos* did not fare so well.

After my time in East LA, I had returned to St. Gregory's Abbey in Shawnee, OK, the monastery where I was a Brother. In about 1974, I called one of the guys in East LA and learned that Mario had been killed. He was one of my more successful tennis students in the schoolyard at Our Lady of Lourdes parish. He was a tall and hefty fellow so I was surprised when Alfred told me that Mario was only 12 years old when he was killed. He got into a fight with some guys from a rival gang. They broke a beer bottle and used it to stab him to death. I was devastated, but there was nothing I could do. I couldn't even get the details straight because in those days long distance phone calls from the monastery were so difficult to make and so expensive that we couldn't talk more than three to five minutes.

In the fall of approximately 1987 or 1988, I received a call from Alfred saying that Hopie had been killed and inviting me to his funeral. I learned that Hopie had borrowed his brother-in-law's car to drive to South Central LA one night. As he stopped at a light, his door was pulled open and he was jerked out of the car. Two black guys bashed him over the head with a brick, took the car, and left him in the gutter.

The police found him and took him to the hospital where he died a couple days later. I was invited to speak and pray at the funeral. As the service broke up and some of us were standing around outside the funeral home, I heard a shot from down the street and a bullet whistled over our heads.

When I called Alfred in about 1995, he said that Fernando had been killed in a bar fight. A couple years later Alfred said that Efren had died of hepatitis C while in prison.

The girls in the Hopie book have mostly moved to San Diego. Christina Almenar ran into me when I was teaching at San Diego City College. She took my College Elementary Algebra class twice, in two different semesters in the late 1990's. She asked me so I baptized her youngest son at La Jolla Cove in about 1999.

The best fruit of my East LA work was Philip. The saddest part is the loss of all of the *cholos* except Alfred who has his own family now. It seems that all of the girls have survived into adulthood and Christina is raising three responsible sons.

In the fall of 1976, I quit the monastery because the Abbot became more and more displeased with everything I did. I settled in San Diego where my years of teaching math for the San Diego Community College District began at City College.

There I befriended *cholos* from 4 different barrios and helped them get into classes at City College. My eight years of work with those guys led to my second book <u>Homeboys in College: Heralds of Progress</u>, published in 1986.

I, too, have my own family now; my magnificent wife and I have raised three wonderful children as I have continued to teach math at another of the San Diego Community College District's campuses, Miramar College. Just Google "Hilary Paul McGuire" to see some of the math teaching improvements I've developed and pictures of my award-winning sculptures. "Justice?" in particular was built with my homies' lives in mind.

I thank God for what little good I have been able to do. From my East LA experience I have developed my personal motto: "There's not much I can do for the world, but what I can, I do".

Made in the USA
Monee, IL
06 February 2020